Caring for
People with
Challenging Behaviors

Caring for People with Challenging Behaviors

Essential Skills and Successful Strategies in Long-Term Care

by

Stephen Weber Long, Ph.D.

Baltimore • London • Sydney

Health Professions Press, Inc.
Post Office Box 10624
Baltimore, Maryland 21285-0624

www.healthpropress.com

Second printing, June 2010

Typeset by Integrated Publishing Solutions, Grand Rapids, Michigan.
Manufactured in the United States of America by
Versa Press, Inc., East Peoria, Illinois.

The information provided in this book is in no way meant to substitute for a medical practitioner's advice or expert opinion. Readers should consult a medical practitioner if they are interested in more information. This book is sold without warranties of any kind, express or implied, and the publisher and author disclaim any liability, loss, or damage caused by the contents of this book.

The case studies in this book are based on the author's experience. These stories are composite accounts that do not represent the lives or experiences of specific individuals, and no implications should be inferred.

Also available:
Health Professions Press offers a companion poster series for free for those who purchase *Caring for People with Challenging Behaviors: Essential Skills and Successful Strategies in Long-Term Care*. Log on to http://healthpropress.com/posterseries to download a PDF file of each of the 12 posters.

Library of Congress Cataloging-in-Publication Data
Long, Stephen Weber.
    Caring for people with challenging behaviors : essential skills and successful strategies in long-term care / by Stephen Weber Long.
        p.   cm.
    Includes bibliographical references and index.
    ISBN 1-878812-91-2 (pbk.)
    1. Nursing home patients—Mental health.   2. Behavior therapy for older people.   I. Title.
RC451.4.N87L66 2005
362.16—dc22

                                                                            2004027643

British Library Cataloguing in Publication data are available from the British Library.

Contents

About the Author

Stephen Weber Long, Ph.D., is a psychologist and psychoanalyst. He received a doctoral degree in clinical psychology from the California School of Professional Psychology in Berkeley/Alameda, California, and a postdoctoral diploma in psychoanalysis and psychotherapy from Adelphi University.

Since 1992, he has been on the Extended Care staff at the Department of Veterans Affairs Medical Center in Northport, New York. As a staff psychologist, he has served as a trainer to caregiving staff, counselor to patients and residents, and consultant to the medical center's supervisors and administrators. Dr. Long is also Adjunct Professor, teaching The Psychology of the Aging, at Adelphi University in Garden City, New York. In addition to teaching, Dr. Long has a private practice in Huntington, New York, which includes consultation and psychotherapy for elders and caregivers.

Acknowledgments

Many people deserve my thanks for their support, guidance, and help in my work and in how this book developed. In early discussions, Judith Ackerhalt, R.N., Ed.D., inspired me with her enthusiasm for ideas from which this book evolved. Later, as the first chapters were written, Pearl Ketover Prilik, D.S.W., gave me invaluable feedback and encouragement. Mary Magnus and Nicole Schmidl of Health Professions Press have been a pleasure to work with in bringing the book through the process of publication. In addition, for many years, Frances Weber, Esq., encouraged and supported me by expressing her confidence in my ability to put ideas in print and by providing clear-headed advice on the business of writing a book.

Finally, I must thank my wife, Helen, my daughter, Elaine, and my son, Adam, for holding me so close in their hearts that I could know the joy of being a husband and a father in many surprising and wonderful ways—ways that motivated and informed my work. They have taught me much.

Introduction

Up to 80% of nursing home residents are described as having moderate to severe behavior problems. In fact, behavior problems are a primary reason for family members deciding to place a loved one in a nursing home.

Many people who begin working in nursing homes are surprised by how often they see, experience, or hear about nursing home residents behaving in difficult ways. It is quite common for residents to yell, shout, scream, resist what staff members try to do with them, and threaten or insult others. It is also fairly common for residents to hit, kick, scratch, or even bite.

In a typical nursing home, addressing these difficulties is a daily part of the staff's work. Many staff members describe dealing with the problem behaviors of residents as the most difficult part of their jobs. These challenging behaviors are sometimes aimed at other residents. Frequently, however, they are aimed at staff.

Caring for People with Challenging Behaviors: Essential Skills and Successful Strategies in Long-Term Care is intended as a guide for nursing home staff to help reduce or eliminate many of residents' typical behavior problems. In this book, the term *behavior problem* refers to any behavior that causes emotional or physical harm. It can be harmful to either the person engaging in the behavior or to someone else. From this point of view, a resident's hostile behavior aimed at someone else is a behavior problem. If a resident's behavior hurts someone else unintentionally, it is still considered a behavior problem. In addition, behaviors related to depression, anxiety, or fear can be problematic.

This book details techniques for successfully addressing such behavior. The effectiveness of these skills is increased when nursing home staff, supervisors, physicians, and administrators have a common understanding of the skills and their importance. The more each staff member supports others' use of the skills, the more effectively the skills can be used by everyone. That is why this book was written for all the people who work in—or will be working in—a nursing home, regardless of job title or role. Whether you are an administrator, a supervisor, or a hands-on caregiver and whether you are a student or a veteran in the field, this book is intended for you.

Caring for People with Challenging Behaviors can also assist mental health professionals who provide consultation to administrators and staff on how nursing home staff may best approach a difficult situation with a particular patient. The principles and skills on which this book is based can be used to create workable treatment plans that address common troubling behaviors.

Caring for People with Challenging Behaviors can be a valuable part of training programs as well. It may be used as the basis for in-service training of staff, supervisors, and administrators. It may also be used as part of the overall training of those who are preparing to begin work in a nursing home.

Often, when a nursing home resident behaves in a troubling way, the resident's behavior is related to an illness such as Alzheimer's disease. Problem behaviors are also sometimes related to other conditions that are more often thought of as mental illnesses, such as depression or schizophrenia. Physical pain or discomfort can also influence a resident to behave in difficult ways. Sometimes a resident's challenging behavior is related to lifelong attitudes, habits, or personality. The methods described in this book are appropriate for use with individuals whose behavior stems from any of these issues.

Whenever a mental or physical illness seems to be contributing to a resident's problem behavior, it is important to seek the advice of appropriately qualified health care professionals. Even in cases when a mental or physical illness is not clearly involved, it is important to consult with trained and experienced health care or mental health care professionals if a behavior problem is persistent. *Caring for People with Challenging Behaviors* is not intended to replace the advice of physicians, nurse practitioners, social workers, psychologists, or any appropriately trained professionals. It is important that the skills described in this book be a central part of treating the problem, regardless of cause. They really are skills for all those who help in the nursing home, whether day-to-day staff, medical specialists, or administrative staff.

Chapter 1 discusses why nursing home residents do what they do. The chapter looks at major influences on behavior through specific examples of how physical functioning, thinking, feeling, existing behavior, and interactions with others can affect what a nursing home resident does. Chapter 1 ends with a discussion of coping with stress. It also describes the importance of increasing the number of pleasant things that happen for us each day as one approach to managing stress.

Chapter 2 looks at ways of encouraging residents' positive behaviors and is illustrated with examples. The chapter is based primarily on three ideas: 1) the more a behavior is reinforced, the more it will occur; 2) the more a resident's positive behavior is reinforced, the less often the resident will engage in difficult behavior; and 3) the resident's experience of interactions with us can be the most valuable source of reinforcing positive behaviors. This chapter shows the steps of active listening, a communication skill to develop an empathic, emotional understanding of residents. Such listening and understanding reinforces many positive behaviors, as it encourages the resident to value his or her relationships with us. Other ways of encouraging positive behaviors are explored as well: allowing residents to make choices and praising, complimenting, or acknowledging positive behavior. The chapter ends by discussing the stress management technique of progressive muscle relaxation.

Chapter 3 is about problem solving. It describes a way of looking at situations—particularly interpersonal interactions (or "relationship situations")—to understand what might trigger or reinforce a resident's difficult behavior. Knowledge of possible triggers and reinforcers can be used to help the resident reduce or eliminate those challenging behaviors. The chapter describes a two-step process for helping reduce frequent demanding or attention-seeking behavior. Chapter 3 contains several examples of staff members successfully using the problem-solving steps to help individuals eliminate or reduce problem behaviors. In addition, the chapter describes how to work with residents in solving problem behavior. Chapter 3 also explains the importance of "holding on," or containing our reactions to residents' difficult behavior. Finally, mental imagery is explored as a stress management technique.

The main point of Chapter 4 is to look more deeply at dealing with the stress related to residents' difficult behavior. The chapter examines how our thinking and feeling can be affected by residents and how our own habits of thinking can cause or add to stress. This chapter is about taking control of our own thoughts and feelings in order to feel less stressed by residents' challenging behavior. How we deal with such stress directly influences how effectively we address the problem behaviors. In addition, Chapter 4 considers how our feelings about residents and difficult behavior can help us in understanding and responding to residents. The chapter concludes by describing a breathing-focused technique for deepening relaxation and stress management.

Chapter 5 examines things that can interfere with the effective use of the techniques described in *Caring for People with Challenging Behaviors*. These factors include our own personal obstacles to effectively using the techniques, the nursing home environment itself, and societal attitudes toward aging and illness. The chapter provides ways of addressing these different obstacles and encourages us to see ourselves, the nursing home, and society as parts of a system—what we do affects the other parts of the system and can promote positive change. Chapter 5 ends by considering the importance of good relationships in managing stress and offers ways to improve relationships.

Chapter 6 is a guide to treatment planning for a resident's behavior problem. The chapter presents a five-step treatment plan guide for individual staff members and a five-step treatment plan guide for interdisciplinary treatment teams. In addition, Chapter 6 describes a way of integrating educational material based on *Caring for People with Challenging Behaviors* into the day-to-day routine of the nursing home, an approach aimed at increasing or deepening all staff members' familiarity with effective techniques for addressing problem behaviors. This approach is also aimed at prevention of many behavior problems because prevention is the best possible treatment. Finally, Chapter 6 can be a useful tool for mental health professionals called on for consultations in cases involving problematic resident behaviors.

For the Reader

Skillful use of the techniques described in *Caring for People with Challenging Behaviors: Essential Skills and Successful Strategies in Long-Term Care* takes practice. These approaches can often be described in simple language. Mastering them, though, is an ongoing process that involves using them in various situations with various people. Throughout the book, descriptions of the techniques are followed by exercises to help readers develop or deepen their mastery of needed skills. These exercises can be useful if the book is read independently or as part of in-service or classroom education. They can promote readers' familiarity with the skills by encouraging active thinking about how to use them. In addition, the exercises may help start or expand classroom discussion.

Helping staff, management, and administration remain familiar with—and deepen their familiarity with—the psychological principles and techniques addressed in this book can be an important part of taking a preventive approach to behavior problems in nursing homes. Even when problem behaviors are not a focus of formal treatment planning, however, it is important to promote the use and understanding of these techniques and principles in ways that become part of a nursing home's culture. Making discussion and awareness of the material addressed in this book routine can promote such a culture.

USE OF THE HANDOUTS AND POSTERS

Advancing discussion and awareness can involve using materials such as the *Caring for People with Challenging Behaviors* poster series (available from Health Professions Press as a free PDF download at http://healthpropress.com/posterseries). The posters can be displayed on a rotating basis, with copies of the first poster hanging in appropriate locations for approximately 4 weeks, copies of the next poster appearing for approximately 4 weeks, and so on. Good places for hanging them include staff break rooms and conference rooms—anywhere staff, treatment planning team members, supervisors, and members of the administration meet.

The posters correspond to some of the book's displays, which can be photocopied for use as handouts. (See Chapter 6 for more information about handout topics.) As soon as a poster is presented, copies of the accompanying handout are distributed to all staff members (including clerical, housekeeping, and food service staff), treatment planning team members, supervisors, and administrators. Handouts may be distributed by immediate supervisors. For example, charge nurses on the different shifts can give handouts to the nursing staff members on their shifts. The facilitator of treatment planning team meetings or another designated person can distribute the handouts to team members present at the meetings. This person also can ensure that members of the administration receive copies.

Supervisors can briefly discuss each handout with staff. Treatment planning team meeting facilitators can do this with the team. Review and discussion of each handout can be added to the agenda of regular meetings attended by members of the nursing home administration as well.

The person who coordinates staff education in the nursing home or another designated person can ensure that posters are rotated and that corresponding handouts are given to supervisors and meeting facilitators. This coordinator may design quizzes with two true-or-false questions based on each handout. Anyone who would like education credits that count toward the nursing home's requirements can complete the quizzes. Completed quizzes on four posters might be considered verification of an hour of continuing education.

Although it is most helpful to display only one poster during each 4-week period, some posters immediately before or after another poster in the series may contain closely related information. In such cases, you might choose to display two to four posters at the same time. In this situation, the handouts that correspond to these posters would be distributed for review and discussion as well.

Using the procedures outlined here, the series of posters and handouts can cycle through each year. This process can be an important part of a nursing home's efforts to meet the educational needs of personnel and the psychological needs of residents.

Dedicated to
Michael, Victor, Karen, Laura, Ellen, and Tina.
You are always with me.

Chapter 1

Why Nursing Home Residents Do What They Do

A number of things influence what a nursing home resident does. This chapter looks at some of the major influences on how nursing home residents act. When interested in reducing or eliminating common troubling behaviors among nursing home residents, it can be helpful to keep in mind some of the reasons why residents act the way that they do. This can help us see which influences on a resident's behavior we can address.

This chapter also raises the idea that it is important to deal effectively with the stress that we are under in order to deal effectively with the challenging behaviors of residents. Therefore, a method for increasing the pleasant things that we do for ourselves is described as one method for coping with stress.

INTERNAL AND EXTERNAL INFLUENCES ON BEHAVIOR

One way to consider causes of troubling behavior is to think about what internal and external things might be triggering behavior. Typically, a behavior problem—that is, something that is harmful physically or emotionally—happens because of internal *and* external factors. In fact, it often is hard to say whether a problem behavior is either completely internal or external. Every behavior problem is likely to have triggers or reinforcers of both types. For example, a resident may have vision trouble and difficulty thinking things through because of impaired brain functioning. These factors might be considered internal problems. However, this person may act confused and irritable in dim or low lighting or when moving from a well-lit area to a dark area. The lighting might be an external cause of the individual's behavior. If staff members cannot discern the combination of internal and external influences, they are not able to aid the resident effectively (e.g., by correcting the lighting). Thus, what staff members do or do not do in response to the resident's behavior could also become an external influence on the resident's difficult behavior. See Display 1.1 and the following sections for more information; in addition, try completing Exercise 1.1.

Physical Functioning

Physical functioning refers to how a person's body works—for example, how well a resident's muscles and joints move or how well he or she breathes. Physical functioning also includes how different areas of a person's brain work, particularly the areas that play an important part in the person's ability to pay attention, to remember new things, to control emotions, to think clearly, to talk, to understand others, and to tell what is and is not real.

A nursing home resident's physical functioning can influence how he or she behaves. Someone with severe arthritis may avoid moving parts of the body that hurt. Someone who has great difficulty with breathing may avoid doing things that could make it harder to breathe. A resident who is decreasingly able to remember new or recent things may talk only about the past. Another resident who believes things are happening that others cannot see or hear may behave in ways that are unusual and apparently unpredictable. The following cases illustrate how various physical issues can affect an individual's behavior.

Mrs. Wells   Mrs. Wells was 92 years old. The pain of the severe arthritis in her hips made it difficult for her to walk, stand, or sit. Even lying in bed in one position for long periods of time was painful. Before she entered a nursing home, Mrs. Wells spent most of the time in bed to avoid further pain. Because this kept her from doing much, she lost a good deal of her overall muscle strength. Mrs. Wells became so frail that when she fell on the way to the bathroom one day at home, she broke her hip. She continued to stay in bed during her time at the nursing home.

In Mrs. Wells' case, the physical condition of arthritis influenced what she did. To avoid further pain, she stayed in bed.

Ms. Quigley   Ms. Quigley was 77 years old. Over a number of years, her ability to breathe declined. Using medications for breathing and oxygen helped, but she still gasped for breath even when she walked only a few steps. Ms. Quigley breathed more easily when she was sitting in a chair beside her bed—so that is what she did most of the day.

Mr. D'Angelo   Mr. D'Angelo was 83 years old. He had what seemed to be Alzheimer's disease. His illness, a type of dementia, interfered with his brain's ability to function well. He could carry on a pretty good conversation, though. He particularly liked talking about baseball and about the major league teams of his

Understanding Causes of Behavior Problems Among Nursing Home Residents

A *behavior problem* is any behavior that is harmful physically or emotionally. It can be harmful to the person doing it or to someone else.

Examples of problem behaviors include a depressed resident withdrawing from other people, an agitated resident shouting repeatedly, an agitated resident hitting someone, or a confused resident wandering from his or her unit.

Causes of behavior problems include internal and external factors that combine to make a behavior happen or keep happening (i.e., trigger or reinforce a behavior).

Sample internal triggers or reinforcers	Sample external triggers or reinforcers
Emotion (e.g., despair, anxiety, fear)	Lack of meaningful activity
Medication	Unpleasant events
Illness (physical or mental)	Unpleasant actions of others
Confusion	Demands of others
Pain or discomfort	Light that is too bright or too dim
Lifelong perceptions	Too much noise
	Being misunderstood by others

Remember: Every problem behavior is likely to have *both* internal and external causes.

Caring for People with Challenging Behaviors: Essential Skills and Successful Strategies in Long-Term Care

Exercise 1.1

Think about an incident in which a nursing home resident engaged in problem behavior. If you cannot think of an incident involving a nursing home resident, think of one in which someone else behaved in a difficult way. Remember, you are thinking about a problem — or difficult — behavior as one that is harmful to someone in some way. It may be harmful to the person engaging in the behavior or to someone else. The harm can be either physical or emotional.

Briefly describe the incident.

Briefly describe the following:

1. What seemed to be some of the internal triggers for the problem behavior?

2. What were some possible external triggers of the problem behavior?

childhood and early adulthood. Mr. D'Angelo liked to watch baseball games on television as well. He wondered, however, about some of the teams that he saw playing. He said that he had never heard of many of these teams. Mr. D'Angelo said he did not know who any of the players were either.

Mr. D'Angelo was not able to remember recent events because of how his apparent Alzheimer's disease affected his brain's physical functioning. An effect on his behavior was that he talked almost solely about the distant past. In addition, he usually did not follow through on things that he had agreed to do, such as going to the nursing home's dining room when told it was mealtime, because he often forgot about agreeing to do anything.

Mr. Siegler   Mr. Siegler was 70 years old. For most of his adult life, he had a serious mental illness that affected his ability to discern reality. At times, he thought that things existed or happened that no one else saw or believed. Mr. Siegler occasionally told nursing home staff members that he was tired of being spied on. He said that the reason he sometimes stood motionless and quiet in his room—and the reason he often did not respond to people talking to him—was that there were microphones all over his room. The microphones, he explained, were taping every sound. The tapes would be used against him, he said. Mr. Siegler's mental illness contributed to his extremely guarded behavior.

Emotions

It is not easy to define the word *emotion*, yet most of us know an emotion when we feel one or see one in another person. We usually recognize happiness, sadness, love, and anger as emotions. Emotions are feelings, a combination of parts of us that are often thought of as mental and physical. Our emotions influence and are influenced by our experience of ourselves and the world around us. A nursing home resident can feel glad or unhappy about certain things that happen in the world. At the same time, a resident who has a tendency to feel glad may also take an optimistic view. Another resident who tends to feel unhappy may be more likely to have a negative view.

Emotions can have a strong influence on what a nursing home resident does—that is, how he or she behaves. A resident who feels embarrassment or shame might avoid others while feeling that way. One who typically feels lonely might frequently look to others for company. Feeling frustrated, annoyed, or angry could make a resident more likely to argue with others or insult them. A resident who is fearful of others may shun social interaction whenever possible. Building on the previously presented cases, the following examples show the effects of emotion on behavior.

Mrs. Wells   Mrs. Wells said that she usually stayed in bed to avoid the pain of the arthritis in her hips, yet she also described feeling depressed. She could not understand why she was depressed; God had granted her a long, full life, she said. It made no sense to her that after such a gift she would feel so miserable. Mrs.

Wells felt sinful and guilty because being depressed seemed ungrateful after the life with which she had been blessed. Feeling guilty made her feel more miserable, which then made her feel more guilty. She was afraid other people would see how bad—how sinful—she was. Feeling ashamed, she did not want other people to see her. This cycle deepened Mrs. Wells' depression.

Mrs. Wells' emotional experience of depression contributed to her isolation. She avoided having visitors, sometimes by telling anyone who came to see her that she was just too tired for a visit. The way that Mrs. Wells acted was very much influenced by her emotions.

Ms. Quigley   For Ms. Quigley, just getting out of bed to sit in the chair at her bedside made it hard for her to catch her breath. She also felt nervous nearly all of the time. Ms. Quigley knew that the medications she took to help her breathe had the side effect of making her feel nervous, yet she said she had been a nervous person her whole life.

Beyond the side effect of her medication, Ms. Quigley said she did not know what made her nervous. She noted that her anxiety worsened when she was alone. She hated being alone, and she hated feeling anxious. As a result, Ms. Quigley often called for help, even for things that she was able to do on her own. At times, she acknowledged that when she felt lonely, she also felt more like she needed help than when she did not feel lonely.

Ms. Quigley's emotional experience of anxiety motivated her to seek help in seemingly unnecessary situations. This action apparently protected her from feeling more alone and anxious.

Mr. D'Angelo   Mr. D'Angelo's dementia made it hard for him to remember new things. Eventually, he had difficulty concentrating or paying attention. He was easily distracted from any task in which he was involved. When he started getting dressed in the mornings, he sometimes left his room while he was not fully dressed. When a staff member helped him get dressed, Mr. D'Angelo would show signs of frustration and annoyance at having to focus on things like getting his socks on, putting his hand in his shirt sleeve, and getting his shirt buttoned. His frustration, annoyance, and growing anger at these things led him to insult whoever was involved in helping him dress. Sometimes these insults were aimed at the other person's race or gender.

Mr. D'Angelo's dementia caused changes that could make him frustrated. In turn, his anger periodically had an unpleasant effect on his behavior.

Mr. Siegler   Part of Mr. Siegler's mental illness was that he was often very afraid. In fact, his strongest and most persistent feeling seemed to be fear. His fear, he said vaguely, came from the threat posed by people "we all know" but about whom he could not say anything more specific. He believed that these people were collecting evidence against him to punish him in some unspeakable way.

For Mr. Siegler, the strength of his fear led him to be withdrawn and guarded; he rarely spoke to or interacted with others.

Thinking

Thinking is often considered a kind of self-talk. Frequently it is seen as what we tell ourselves, usually silently in our own minds. Self-talk can be about many topics: ourselves, others, our experience of the world around us, and our beliefs.

How a nursing home resident thinks can have a major influence on how that person behaves. For example, if a resident thinks that he or she is bad and feels guilty, that individual might tend toward isolation to avoid having others see the badness. Another resident who considers being alone as a terrible thing may often try to secure the company of others. If a resident thinks that other people are always trying to control what he or she does, that person may act uncooperatively or combatively in struggling against the experience of being controlled. Yet another person living in a nursing home might think that others would disapprove of his or her thoughts and feelings. If this individual expects punishment from others because of these thoughts and feelings, he or she might try to avoid doing things that would disclose them. The continuing cases further indicate how thinking can affect behavior.

Mrs. Wells   In her depression, Mrs. Wells tended to think of herself as being completely bad and sinful. She thought that if other people were with her, they would see how bad and sinful she was. Mrs. Wells avoided others to avoid being treated as she believed she deserved—that is, with cruelty and neglect.

How Mrs. Wells thought affected the way that she acted. Her thinking about herself and how she thought she deserved to be treated contributed to her self-imposed isolation.

Ms. Quigley   Ms. Quigley was filled with anxiety when she was alone. While alone, she kept thinking that something terrible was going to happen and no one would be there to help her. As a result, Ms. Quigley tried to think of ways to make people come to her so she would not be alone.

Even when people were with Ms. Quigley, she continuously thought about when they would leave her. She thought of how unbearable being alone would be. As a result, Ms. Quigley created ways to make people stay with her.

These thoughts contributed to Ms. Quigley's behavior. They led her to insist on getting help with things that she could do independently.

Mr. D'Angelo   Mr. D'Angelo often said that other people were trying to make him do what they wanted him to do. He thought people wanted him to stop doing what he preferred and to start doing something else. Occasionally, he said he knew that he was not thinking clearly and often did not make the best decisions. He said he was losing himself, losing the person he had always experienced himself to be, losing control over what was happening to him.

Mr. D'Angelo's thoughts apparently influenced him to act uncooperatively as a way of asserting himself. They moved him to resist feeling that his dwindling sense of himself was being overwhelmed. These thoughts led to verbal attacks on staff members who saw themselves as only trying to help him. To Mr. D'Angelo's way of thinking, however, he was not attacking them; he was defending himself.

Mr. Siegler   Mr. Siegler thought that if others knew what he was thinking and feeling they would attack him. He thought of how they would reprimand or punish him. Mr. Siegler tried to keep anything he did or said from showing what he thought or felt. He did this to avoid the attacks, the reprimands, and the punishment. Thinking the way that he did contributed to Mr. Siegler's acting in ways that isolated him from others. Only rarely was he able to let his guard down enough with anyone to say how fearful he was and how he expected to be abused.

Behavior that Leads to Further Behavior

Behavior is frequently thought of as action. It is something that is done. People's behavior is often categorized as the things they do that can be seen or observed by others. Walking, talking, sitting, eating, laughing, and crying are all examples of behavior.

Our own behavior has an influence on the things we do next. For example, if a person takes a long walk, that might trigger him or her to sit down. In a nursing home environment, a resident's behavior can have an impact on what else he or she does. A resident who is withdrawn and stays in bed may express decreasing interest in getting out of bed. While the person remains in bed, he or she will not have experiences that could trigger and reinforce behaviors other than staying in bed. For this resident, staying in bed would contribute to increased time spent in bed. A resident who engages in few self-care activities may call for help frequently. A person who resists the help of staff members may spend more time doing things independently. Another resident who rarely speaks to others may continue to spend most of his or her time in solitude. The continuing cases present such examples of behavior further influencing behavior.

Mrs. Wells   As noted, Mrs. Wells stayed in bed not only because of her arthritis pain but also because she wanted to avoid having visitors. By behaving in this way, Mrs. Wells was severely limiting her possibilities of experiencing the everyday, pleasant events that could have reduced or eliminated her depression and its negative impact on her overall physical and mental functioning. For example, by staying in bed, Mrs. Wells did not see sunsets. She was not able to see children playing, birds flitting about in the trees, people walking by, or slow-moving clouds against a blue sky. The possible positive effects of such things on her emotional life and general health were lost to Mrs. Wells as she remained in bed.

Ms. Quigley   It seemed that the more Ms. Quigley avoided doing things for herself, the more she called for help. The less she did, the more she said she needed help doing. Ms. Quigley's helpless behavior appeared to diminish her independence and contribute to her help-seeking behavior.

Mr. D'Angelo   For a while, when Mr. D'Angelo resisted things that staff members tried to do with him, he said things such as, "I don't need any help!" or "Don't I have any say in what is going on around here?!" He would frequently insist that he could do things on his own and make his own decisions. When he was asked why he so frequently clashed with staff, Mr. D'Angelo said it was the only way to keep from being taken over. As his dementia progressed, Mr. D'Angelo's ability to use words and think clearly decreased. He became more likely to resist staff physically—by pulling away, hitting, or kicking.

When Mr. D'Angelo was verbally or physically combative, this behavior seemed to escalate. His resisting behavior seemed to contribute to further resisting behavior.

Mr. Siegler   Mr. Siegler behaved in ways that isolated him from others. He stayed to himself and rarely said anything to anyone. As a result, the things he thought about—such as being spied on and being abused for what he thought or felt—could not be changed by comparing his experience with what others actually said or did. Engaging in isolating behavior contributed to Mr. Siegler's continued isolating behavior.

Interactions with Other People

During interactions, the things that one person does or says influence what others do or say. In other words, what people do affects what other people do.

The behavior of nursing home residents is often influenced by their experience of the behavior of the people around them. For example, a resident who is told by others "don't talk that way" when speaking of feeling despair may, under certain circumstances, withdraw from social interaction. This may be most true when the person feels despair most of the time. The resident may interpret "don't talk that way" as an admonition that the greater part of his or her current experience of life is not acceptable.

Another resident who often calls for assistance and is told not to call so much may react by calling more often. This can be particularly the case if, for example, the resident feels helplessly alone and fears that those who say not to call so much will leave the resident alone more often. Feeling more loneliness and fear, the resident's calling for help might increase.

A staff member will often help a resident with activities such as showering, getting dressed, eating, standing, or getting into bed. Sometimes the resident will react to this help with anger. Although the angry reaction may seem unprovoked, it is important to recognize that the response happened during an interaction. Despite a staff member's best intentions, there will be times when a resident will experience an interaction differently from what the staff member expected or thinks is justified or makes sense. Uncooperative, combative, threatening, and withdrawing behaviors are likely to be influenced by interactions between or among people. To fully understand these behaviors in a way that can help to reduce or eliminate them, we need to work to understand residents' experiences of the interactions which influence the difficult behaviors. The continuing cases exemplify this principle.

Mrs. Wells   Mrs. Wells' daughter visited her at least every week. A common scenario follows:

Mrs. Wells said that she was too tired for a visit, and her daughter replied, "You can't be tired, Mother. You're in bed all the time, even though you shouldn't be." When Mrs. Wells said that she felt miserable, her daughter stated, "You just have to stop wallowing in self-pity, Mother. Stop thinking about everything being wrong." Then, when Mrs. Wells became tearful and cried, her daughter said, "Mother, please stop; I can't bear to see you cry."

Mrs. Wells felt worse—that is, more depressed—during and after these visits than before. She believed that her daughter could not tolerate her, that her daughter was reacting to Mrs. Wells' being bad and doing, thinking, and feeling the wrong things: Her being in bed was wrong, her thinking about her problems was wrong, and her crying was wrong.

Mrs. Wells' experience of interactions with her daughter reinforced her feelings of being alone in how she felt, of hopelessness, and of being a bad person. It reinforced her desire to avoid people so she could avoid their reaction to how bad and how sinful she was. It reinforced her behaving in ways aimed at keeping to herself.

Ms. Quigley   A new nursing assistant, Jen, was assigned to work with Ms. Quigley. Each day for a week, Jen hurried to Ms. Quigley's room whenever Ms. Quigley used the call bell or cried out for help. Ms. Quigley called often for help with things such as finding her glasses when they were on the table next to her or being told what kind of soup was on the lunch tray in front of her.

It was impossible for Jen to help all of the other residents assigned to her, to do everything else she needed to do, while constantly running to Ms. Quigley. She spoke with her supervisor, who asked the attending physician, Dr. Pasignine, to speak to Ms. Quigley about her attention-seeking behavior.

Dr. Pasignine explained to Ms. Quigley that the staff wanted to do the things Ms. Quigley needed them to do. However, she said, Ms. Quigley had to realize that she was not the only person for whom the staff members offered care. The doctor asked Ms. Quigley to call only when she really needed help.

Ms. Quigley said that she did only call when she needed help. She said that nobody seemed to understand just how sick she was and how much help she needed. They did not realize, she explained, that when she was left on her own, she was frightened about how much she needed someone to help her. As she talked, her breathing became shallower and quicker. After Dr. Pasignine told her that staff members would do their best to ensure that Ms. Quigley got the care she needed, Ms. Quigley's breathing improved. Unfortunately, following the doctor's visit, Ms. Quigley called for help even more often than she had before.

When a staff member asked about her increasing calls for help, Ms. Quigley explained that following Dr. Pasignine's visit, she felt even more anxious and fearful. Ms. Quigley said that maybe Dr. Pasignine would do what she could for her, but the doctor often was not available. Ms. Quigley said that she could only feel more certain that no one would come to her when she really needed help. Apparently, Ms. Quigley's experience of the interaction with Dr. Pasignine had a significant impact on Ms. Quigley's behavior.

Mr. D'Angelo   Tara, a nursing assistant, went to Mr. D'Angelo's room to help him dress. At first he said, "Okay," and was pleasant when Tara said she was going to help him get dressed. As Tara was getting clothes from the dresser drawers, she asked Mr. D'Angelo to get out of bed. He did not respond, and the following interaction took place:

Tara went to the bed and tried to coax Mr. D'Angelo to sit up by taking his hand and saying, "Okay, here we go."

Mr. D'Angelo pulled his hand away and cried, "What are you doing?"

"Mr. D'Angelo, it's time for you to get up," Tara responded.

"What are you talking about? I'm not getting up," Mr. D'Angelo said crossly.

Tara said, "Mr. D'Angelo, you can't stay in bed all day. The doctor said it's not good for you to be in bed all day."

"Oh, the doctor said that?" Mr. D'Angelo said.

Tara continued, "That's right. So here, let me help you sit up." Tara held out her hand to Mr. D'Angelo.

"What do you want now?" Mr. D'Angelo asked impatiently.

Because things were not going well, Tara decided to let Mr. D'Angelo stay where he was. She decided to help him get ready for the day a little later.

Mr. D'Angelo's lack of cooperation was not unusual. In the past, he was more likely to argue, complain, or insult others as he resisted help. Gradually, though, he resisted by not responding to requests, pulling away, and making brief statements such as, "What are you doing?" This change in the way he resisted seemed to show that his dementia was progressing, apparently affecting the parts of his brain that are involved in the more complicated thinking that he had previously used to express his arguments or complaints. Dementia's progression also appeared to make it more difficult for him to remember things that were said or done just minutes earlier. At this point, resisting or fussing seemed to be the only ways for him to express what he had previously expressed in words. Mr. D'Angelo struggled to retain some control. He experienced his interaction with Tara as an instance of his not having a say in what was happening to him.

Mr. Siegler   Ben, a new recreational therapist at the nursing home, found Mr. Siegler in his usual spot—his room. Ben said hello, introduced himself, and told Mr. Siegler which therapeutic recreational events were coming up that day. When Mr. Siegler did not respond, Ben asked if Mr. Siegler wanted to join any of the day's events. Mr. Siegler did not answer. He just stood in the middle of the room, looking at the floor.

"You're not going to stand there looking at the floor all day, are you?" Ben said good-naturedly.

Mr. Siegler said nothing. He just stood there silently.

Ben said, "Well, okay, I'll go now. But if you want to join an activity just come and do it. We'll be glad to have you." Then Ben left.

It is hard to evaluate Mr. Siegler's experience of the interaction with Ben. Mr. Siegler often said or did little because he did not want to reveal what he was feeling or thinking. Only when he felt safe with someone was Mr. Siegler able to describe his fears. It typically took repeated, brief contact with a person before Mr. Siegler could feel that safe.

Interacting with Ben was new to Mr. Siegler. Being approached by a stranger likely heightened Mr. Siegler's fear and suspicion and contributed to his silence and inactivity.

COPING WITH STRESS

From your own work in a nursing home, the examples of Mrs. Wells, Ms. Quigley, Mr. D'Angelo, and Mr. Siegler may seem familiar. You may recognize that the things nursing home residents do often provoke a variety of reactions in nursing home staff. Some of our reactions as staff members—whether they are feelings such as frustration, fear, anger, or depression—will, if they are strong enough, cause us stress.

Working in a nursing home is not the only source of our stress, either. At times, we feel stress related to family and other obligations. All of these sources add to our overall level of stress, making it difficult to cope effectively with any particular stressful situation—such as dealing with a resident's problem behavior.

Justine's Experience

Justine, a licensed practical nurse (LPN) who worked at a nursing home, was a single mother with a 7-year-old daughter, Katie. Justine's own mother had recently had a stroke, and Justine visited her daily at the hospital.

Before work one morning, Justine had an argument during a telephone conversation with her ex-husband. They argued about which parent would pick up Katie after school and take her to Justine's sister's house while Justine visited her mother at the hospital. Although her ex-husband finally agreed to pick up their daughter that afternoon, the argument had taken so much time that Justine was afraid that she would be late for work.

When Justine was about to go out the door with Katie, she remembered that she needed to pay for her daughter's school lunch program. While quickly writing a check, she noticed that her checking account was overdrawn.

As Justine was leaving Katie at the school's early morning child care program, the principal greeted her. The principal wanted to talk about Katie's having pushed another child down during recess the day before. The principal was concerned, she said, because Justine's daughter had done similar things a number of times recently. After promising to call for an appointment to discuss all of this at another time, Justine drove to work. She was sure that she would be late.

Justine was really only 5 minutes late. She was relieved when no one seemed concerned. In fact, her supervisor gave her a warm, "Hello, Justine." A moment later, her friend, another LPN, said, "Hey, girlfriend. I'm calling the take-out place early to have some food delivered for lunchtime. Do you want me to order your usual?" The unit secretary looked up to say hello and added how nice Justine's new hairstyle looked.

With the way the day had started, Justine had been nearly ready to scream or cry when she arrived at work. She gratefully considered how the brief pleasant interactions with her supervisor, her friend, and the unit secretary were just what she needed. Although not completely over the difficulties of the morning, Justine did feel a little less tense and upset. She appreciated the slight positive shift in her mood.

Having to interact with Mr. D'Angelo without those small pleasant events might have been the last straw for Justine. Without the boost from those inter-actions, she might have reacted in a less-than-positive way. As it turned out, she effectively responded to Mr. D'Angelo when he said, "What are you doing? Get the hell outta here!" while turning his head to avoid the medications she was try-ing to give him. Justine responded by gently saying that she would come back a little later to see if he was ready then for his medications.

It also helped her cope with Ms. Quigley. While Justine was giving medica-tions to Ms. Quigley's next-door neighbors, Ms. Quigley stuck her head out her door three times in 15 minutes to ask, "When is it time for my medication?" Jus-tine answered her quietly each time, first saying that Ms. Quigley's medication was planned to be given in the next 20 minutes, then saying the next 15 minutes, and finally saying, "Right now, Ms. Quigley. Here you go."

The effects of Justine's brief positive interactions with other staff members—simply small, pleasant events—were not major. However, they helped balance the stressful experiences of that morning. This made it more likely that Justine would effectively address difficult situations that might arise. Applying the following method of using small, pleasant events can help manage stress.

Using Pleasant Events to Manage Stress

Pleasant events are activities that you enjoy. They can be small, everyday things. Having someone smile at you, preparing a tasty meal, laughing, or taking a walk are examples of pleasant events for some people. Although these events are small, having many throughout the day can be very helpful in counteracting stress.

Setting a Goal   How many pleasant activities should you have each day? Only you can decide the answer to this question. It may be good to strive for a bal-ance between the number of pleasant activities that you experience and the more difficult tasks that you are obligated to do. A sign that you have reached this bal-ance is that you do not feel burned out or overly stressed.

The research of psychologist Peter Lewinsohn and his colleagues suggests that the average adult has between 5 and 10 pleasant activities a day. If you are hav-ing fewer than 5 pleasant activities a day, you may decide to increase the number of enjoyable things that you do. You might consider the range of 5–10 a guide. If you are having as many as 10 pleasant events per day, you are not likely to be overindulging. Also, you may need additional pleasant events during particularly stressful times. When your circumstances are notably stressful, it is good to plan for more than 5 to 10 pleasant activities each day. This will foster a balance that will help protect your mental and physical health and will positively affect your work and relationships with others. Keep in mind that working in a nursing home is likely (at least occasionally) to put you in circumstances that are notably more stressful than average. For example, coping with the deaths of those with whom you have daily contact is a frequent aspect of working in nursing homes. It is not a usual aspect of work in most other settings.

Increasing Your Pleasant Events   The following sections outline a method for increasing the number of pleasant events that you have each day.

Making Your List of Pleasant Events   Use the Top 10 Pleasant Events List (or "Top 10 List") in the appendix at the end of the book to make a list of 10 things you enjoy doing. Make sure that you include activities that you can realistically do. For example, a 2-month cruise to faraway places is less realistic than going to a favorite neighborhood coffee shop, taking a walk, reading, or sitting quietly for a few minutes. See Display 1.2 for a list of things many people find enjoyable.

In addition to being realistic, choose activities that you do not already do very much. Your list will then include the top 10 "do-able" pleasant activities that you can do on a regular basis. Rank the items, putting the most pleasant, do-able infrequent activity at the top of the list.

Tracking Pleasant Events   Over the course of a week, use the Pleasant Events Tracking Form in the appendix to track how many days each Top 10 activity happens. By using the tracking form, you will see how many of your Top 10 activities you actually engage in each day.

Revising Your Top 10 List   After a week of tracking your Top 10 List, determine if it needs some changes. Were you unable to do a particular activity? Would a different activity be more realistic? Use the New Top 10 List of Pleasant Events form in the appendix to make a revised list. Replace anything on your original list that you were not able to do.

Tracking Your New Top 10   Over the course of the next week, use the Pleasant Events Tracking Form in the appendix again. See how many of these pleasant activities you engage in each day.

Continuing with Pleasant Events   Each week you can revise your list by following the preceding two steps. Eventually, you may find that making a list is unnecessary because you have learned to include enough pleasant events in your life. However, if you begin to feel overwhelmed, tense, or depressed or begin to notice any other signs of stress, it can be helpful to once again follow this method for increasing pleasant events.

Planning   Planning ahead can help when you are working on increasing your number of enjoyable activities. If an activity involves taking a trip or going out for an evening, you might have to think ahead, for example, to plan your route, buy tickets for an event, or arrange for a babysitter. If an activity cuts into time for activities that you do not enjoy, such as housecleaning or shopping, you will need to make plans for tending to these chores.

Some enjoyable activities are easier to work into a busy schedule and require less planning. On full days, it may be good to do those less complicated pleasant

Pleasant Events

Pleasant events are activities that you enjoy. They can be very small things, such as getting a hug, watching the sun set, or watching a favorite television program.

Experiencing small, pleasant events throughout the day can help us deal with stress. The positive effects of frequent pleasant activities can help balance the negative impact of stressful circumstances.

Examples of Events Many People Find Pleasant*

Laughing	Breathing clean air	Spending time with friends
Spending time in the country	Kissing	Sitting in the sun
Hearing that I am loved	Having a lively talk	Having a good meal
Wearing clean clothes	Being with someone I love	Amusing people
Watching people	Being with pets	Having sex
Reading	Driving	Having spare time
Smiling at people	Seeing old friends	Being relaxed
Expressing my love	Complimenting someone	Going to a party
Being seen as attractive	Viewing wild animals	Sleeping well
Being complimented	Thinking about people I like	Learning
Planning or organizing	Having a frank discussion	Speaking clearly
Doing a project my way	Seeing beautiful scenery	Doing a job well

If you are having 10 such experiences per day, it is unlikely that you are overindulging. If you are having fewer than 5 pleasant events per day, you may be at risk for suffering the negative mental and physical effects of stress.

When life is more stressful than usual for you, it is a good idea to plan to have more than the average number of pleasant activities each day.

*Source: Lewinsohn, Muñoz, Youngren, & Zeiss (1986).

Caring for People with Challenging Behaviors: Essential Skills and Successful Strategies in Long-Term Care
© 2005 Stephen Weber Long. Published by Health Professions Press, Inc. (http://www.healthpropress.com).
All rights reserved.

activities. Also, once you have planned a pleasant activity, you might face pressure from others to give up your plan. Remember that it is usually okay to say, "Sorry, but I have other plans during that time."

SUMMARY

Chapter 1 looked at five major influences on the behavior of nursing home residents:

1. Physical functioning: A person's body (including the brain) functioning contributes to behavior.

2. Emotions: How someone feels emotionally is a primary influence on the way that he or she acts.

3. Thinking: The way that an individual thinks about or understands what is happening to or around him or her affects behavior.

4. Behavior: Some behaviors lead to other behaviors, and some behaviors seem to perpetuate themselves.

5. Interactions with other people: The way that a person experiences interactions with other people is a significant influence on his or her behavior.

The chapter also emphasized the importance of remembering that every behavior problem seen in nursing home residents is likely to have internal and external causes.

Finally, Chapter 1 raised the idea that our stress level can affect how well we are able to cope with difficult situations in a nursing home. Increasing our number of small, daily pleasant activities is an approach to managing stress.

Encouraging Positive Behavior

One of the most significant influences on the behavior of a nursing home resident is external: It is how we, the people around the resident, behave, particularly how we behave toward the resident in our interactions with him or her. Through our actions, we can encourage residents to behave in positive ways. This is important when our goal is to decrease or eliminate problem behaviors. The more often a nursing home resident is engaged in positive behaviors, the less often that person will be engaging in problem behaviors. In fact, the best way to reduce problem behaviors is to encourage, trigger, or reinforce positive behaviors. The single most important source of encouragement or reinforcement for positive behavior is us, the nursing home staff upon whom residents must depend. This chapter looks at three ways of encouraging and reinforcing positive behaviors: engaging in active listening; allowing choices; and using praise, compliments, and acknowledgment.

Chapter 2 also continues to focus on coping with stress. This chapter describes the stress management technique of progressive muscle relaxation.

ENGAGING IN ACTIVE LISTENING

The way that we communicate with nursing home residents can encourage positive behavior. One significantly useful set of communication skills is often called *active listening.* When we use active listening most effectively, we become tuned in to the thoughts and feelings of the person to whom we are listening. When we use this technique, we are able to increase our empathic understanding of nursing home residents. Effective use of active listening can communicate to a resident that we hear what that person needs us to hear. It lets that person know that we can tolerate and accept who the resident is and what the resident feels or experiences.

Generally, the more people experience being understood in this way (frequently described as *feeling emotionally supported*), the more positive their behaviors become. This type of emotional social support is associated with mental and physical health as well as overall quality of life. It appears to be a basic human need, much like an essential nutrient in its effects on physical, psychological, and behavioral functioning. When it is in short supply, the ill effects of "undernourishment" become increasingly evident. Behavioral, psychological, and physical problems are likely to worsen, especially in those who are most vulnerable due to predisposition, stress, or illness. These are the people who most need the "nutrient" of accurate emotional attunement.

Unfortunately, problem behaviors frequently make others less inclined to provide close, accepting support. Often, we are more likely to respond by withdrawing from or avoiding a person who engages in challenging behavior. However, this can result in a negative cycle of worsening behavior and further withdrawal or avoidance.

By using active listening, we can help meet residents' needs for basic human emotional support, which in turn will promote residents' positive behaviors. When we use active listening, we stop what we are doing and show that we are paying attention to the person. We make eye contact, to the degree the person is able to tolerate. We use body language to show that we are listening: we nod, sit, crouch, or bend down to be at eye level with people who are in wheelchairs, geriatric chairs, or beds. We show that we are listening by saying things such as, "Hmm," "Uh-huh," and "Oh." We also summarize and restate what the person to whom we are listening says or feels.

Offering advice, making suggestions, correcting the speaker's misperceptions, or telling the speaker what to do are not parts of active listening. Although these behaviors may be important at times, they should come only after we use active listening, if at all. Typically, it is best to spend more time actively listening to residents than giving advice, making suggestions, correcting misperceptions, or telling them what to do. Frequently, our being truly present and accepting is of greater importance than our attempting to solve a resident's problems or to make a resident's troubling emotions go away. See Display 2.1 for a summary of active listening and the following case studies for illustrations of this skill.

Mrs. Ortiz

At age 83, Mrs. Ortiz was very forgetful. Whenever she left her room, she could not remember how to get back. Sometimes she was found sitting in someone else's room. She frequently misplaced things and lost money. Mrs. Ortiz liked to have a few dollars handy, though. She agreed with her treatment team and family's decision to give her a small amount of cash each week.

Active Listening

The emotional support felt by being listened to can be an important part of the care that we provide to residents. It can help increase positive behaviors and decrease difficult behaviors.

Active listening techniques:

1. Show the person that you are listening. Stop anything else you are doing. Make eye contact (as much as the person is able to tolerate). Show that you are paying attention by doing things such as nodding your head or saying "Hmm," "Uh-huh," and "Oh."

2. Listen to what the person says and what the person communicates nonverbally. Accept whatever feelings are presented. Avoid trying to correct the person's point of view.

3. Restate in your own words what the person seems to be expressing by words or actions. As you listen, occasionally summarize the most important part of what the person has just said. Name the feelings that the person has expressed. Restate the reasons that the person believes are behind these feelings.

4. Make suggestions, give advice, reassure, or offer a different way of looking at things only after engaging in active listening — if at all.

Use active listening often. It can be helpful with all nursing home residents, especially those who are agitated, confused, or depressed.

Caring for People with Challenging Behaviors: Essential Skills and Successful Strategies in Long-Term Care

One day, Mrs. Ortiz used all of her cash to buy some toiletries. Later, when Phil, the staff social worker, asked Mrs. Ortiz how she was doing, she looked up from her wheelchair and said, "They keep taking my money."

"You've lost some money," Phil responded.

"I didn't lose anything. These people here took it. They take *everything*!" Mrs. Ortiz said as she shook her fist in the air.

"I don't think anyone took your money, Mrs. Ortiz. You spent it this morning," Phil said.

"You don't think! You don't think!" Mrs. Ortiz said, raising her voice and shaking both fists at Phil. There were tears in her eyes.

"It can be pretty hard when no one seems to believe you," Phil stated, voicing what he thought was Mrs. Ortiz's point of view.

"That's right," said Mrs. Ortiz putting down her fists. "They take all of your things and then cover up for each other," she continued.

"You're having all of your things taken and nobody is admitting it," Phil restated what Mrs. Ortiz just said.

"Oh, dear, I miss my things," Mrs. Ortiz said, crying quietly. "I used to have such nice things."

Phil crouched down to eye level with Mrs. Ortiz and held her hand. "It's very sad, not having your things," he said. In so doing, Phil named the feeling that he believed Mrs. Ortiz was experiencing and restated her apparent explanation for her behavior.

"You're such a nice man," Mrs. Ortiz said, patting Phil's hand.

"Thank you. I like talking with you, too," Phil said.

After a moment, Phil said he had to go but that he would stop by again later in the day.

"Oh, I'd like that, dear," Mrs. Ortiz responded. "But what about my money?"

"Maybe we can talk more about that when I see you again," Phil answered.

"Okay," said Mrs. Ortiz.

This situation started out a bit rocky. When Phil tried to convince Mrs. Ortiz that things were not as she saw them, she became agitated. Phil de-escalated the situation by using the active listening techniques of stating what he thought Mrs. Ortiz believed and restating what he heard her say. He used body language to show that he was listening by crouching down to eye level and holding Mrs. Ortiz's hand. Phil also used the active listening technique of naming the feeling he thought Mrs. Ortiz was having when he said, "It's very sad. . . ."

Phil effectively encouraged Mrs. Ortiz's positive behavior of talking with him about what was happening from her point of view. Although what Mrs. Ortiz was saying about others seemed untrue, talking about her beliefs, point of view, and feelings were positive behaviors. Phil's use of active listening also encouraged Mrs. Ortiz to speak less loudly and to cease using threatening hand gestures.

It is not unusual for a nursing home resident to become agitated when someone else denies what he or she believes is real. When a resident is very confused and agitated, trying to convince him or her of our version of the truth—that is, trying to orient the person to reality—will not usually reassure the person. More likely, it will result in the resident's feeling more confused. Then the resident often becomes determined to fight against the confusion by insisting on the rightness of his or her point of view and to fight against us. If a nursing home resident is more prone to feeling victimized than confused, he or she may react to attempts to correct misperceptions as further victimization. The person's experience can be that his or her reality is denied, that his or her ability to think or even to see things plainly is being attacked. Frequently, the more attacked a resident feels, the more inclined he or she is to counterattack in defense. Phil avoided these possible problems by using active listening.

When Phil was first learning to use active listening, it was uncomfortable for him. It seemed to him that reflecting back, restating, echoing, or mirroring what a resident said was often lying. When Phil was learning active listening techniques, he would not have been able to say, "You're having all of your things taken and nobody is admitting it" in response to Mrs. Ortiz's statement that "They take all of your things and then cover up for each other." Back then, Phil would have thought that such a response would amount to agreement. It was not until he started trying the techniques of restating and rephrasing that he understood their value. Phil eventually recognized that using these listening techniques did not necessarily mean that he agreed with the words he used when he restated or rephrased what he heard.

As he used active listening over time, Phil more fully realized that something true typically underlies the specific words used in an interaction such as the one with Mrs. Ortiz. For example, Mrs. Ortiz *did* feel sad. Although staff members were not taking the things that she named, things were being taken from her. That is, her physical and cognitive functions were increasingly being taken from her. All of this was unmistakably true, unmistakably real. This was the underlying truth that Phil would not have been able to hear or understand if he had tried to defend himself and others from Mrs. Ortiz's accusations instead of engaging in active listening. If Phil had argued with Mrs. Ortiz about the details of her comments, he would not have truly heard what she was saying. If Phil had avoided Mrs. Ortiz to escape being accused or treated like an accomplice, he would not have heard her. If Phil had reacted in these ways instead of actively listening to Mrs. Ortiz, an opportunity to provide care for her mental health would have been missed.

Behind the specific words used by a distressed or angry resident are feelings and thoughts that are very real. Sometimes illness, personality, stress, or simply lack of practice can make it difficult for people to bear these strong feelings and accurately put them into words. The words that residents use to express feelings might not be literally true, but the same can be said of all of us. For example, when we say something like, "My heart is breaking," we do not mean that our heart is physically being broken. We can, though, be speaking of an experience that to us is very real and difficult to describe in any other words.

Active listening allows us to hear the deeper meaning of what nursing home residents say. With practice, active listening can help us better discern what a resident is feeling by putting us in touch with those feelings. Such empathy or emotional understanding on our part can encourage positive resident behaviors. This is what happened between Phil and Mrs. Ortiz.

When Phil went back to visit Mrs. Ortiz later that day, she again spoke of her money being stolen and how she wanted it replaced. Phil did not make plans with her about getting money to replace what she said was stolen. He did not try to convince her that it had not been stolen. He did not remind her that she had memory problems and that a plan was already in place to ensure she had spending money every week. All of these approaches were tried with Mrs. Ortiz in the past. They usually resulted in her shouting accusations and shaking her fists; once, Mrs. Ortiz even hit a staff member.

Phil made listening his primary way of being with Mrs. Ortiz. As other staff members followed Phil's example, Mrs. Ortiz's episodes of angry, agitated behavior decreased and became rare. Generally, after less than a minute of active listening, Mrs. Ortiz ceased speaking of things being taken from her. Instead, she would begin reminiscing about things such as how difficult it had been to manage her household finances during hard times as a young mother. She would then speak of her children and her husband and of how much she loved them. Mrs. Ortiz would often mention how much the person using active listening reminded her of her husband or one of her children.

Ms. Chen

Ms. Chen was 77 years old. She had lived in psychiatric units much of her life before coming to the nursing home. She seemed to have no physical disabilities; however, she was incontinent of bowel and bladder and liked to use a wheelchair even though she could walk. Ms. Chen's psychiatric condition was usually stable, but her abilities to think clearly and to interact with others had not been good for many years.

Reverend White, who frequently visited the nursing home, was passing Ms. Chen in the hallway. He was on his way to a meeting.

"Run me over! Run me over! Run me over, why don't you!" shouted Ms. Chen, staring directly at the reverend.

"Run you over?" Reverend White asked as he stopped and looked at Ms. Chen.

"You people are all alike—always busy, busy. Never any time to make sure you're not running people over," Ms. Chen continued.

"You want me to have time for you," Reverend White said, restating what he thought Ms. Chen was saying.

"Nobody has any respect for rank and privilege around here. I'm not only wealthy; my mother is royalty. My father is, too. But we don't like to talk about that."

"You aren't being treated the way you should be," Reverend White said, summarizing Ms. Chen's statements.

"That's what I'm saying," Ms. Chen replied quietly. Then she said, "I think it's lunchtime," as she began pushing herself toward the dining room, leaving Reverend White.

Reverend White used a few active listening techniques in his interaction with Ms. Chen. He showed that he was paying attention to Ms. Chen by stopping and looking at her. When he restated and summarized what he thought she was saying, he showed that he was paying attention. In turn, Ms. Chen's shouting stopped. Apparently, his paying attention to Ms. Chen—and letting her know that he was doing so by using active listening—encouraged her more positive, quiet behavior. The reverend's continuing to show her attention during this interaction seemed to reinforce the more quiet behavior, too. Ms. Chen had frequently shouted at people, but once staff members started regularly using active listening before she shouted, her episodes of shouting became rare.

The interaction between Reverend White and Ms. Chen was brief. There was not enough time for Reverend White to do much, as he was expected at a meeting. Yet, the discussion also ended because Ms. Chen seemed to want it to. Reverend White showed that he was paying attention to that wish by not insisting that Ms. Chen say more. He did not try to find out more about Ms. Chen or to make small talk, as he could do those things another time. Regardless, he probably found out more about Ms. Chen by paying attention to what she did and when she did it rather than by asking her directly.

Brief, frequent interactions are often the most that people with severe mental illness are able to tolerate without becoming anxious, more confused, or agitated. Being with people with severe mental illness frequently means interacting with them only as much as they are able to tolerate. However, over time, gradual improvement is possible. Improvement can be seen in increased positive behaviors that are encouraged by active listening—behaviors such as longer interactions with others and conversations containing fewer signs of confused thinking or delusions.

Ms. Zabransky

Ms. Zabransky, age 49, had multiple sclerosis. She needed help with all of her routine activities of daily living.

Jill, a nursing assistant, responded to Ms. Zabransky's call bell.

"It's about time you got here! I could be lying on the floor dead before you decided to come!" Ms. Zabransky yelled.

Jill said, "You feel like you've been waiting a very long time."

"I don't FEEL like anything. I WAS waiting a long f——ing time," Ms. Zabransky growled.

"You're pretty angry," Jill responded.

"Damn right, I'm angry. Wouldn't you be if you had to rely on people you can't rely on?" Ms. Zabransky went on.

"It's not easy to depend on other people when they might not be there when you need them," said Jill.

"That's right," Ms. Zabransky said, no longer yelling or growling.

"What can I do for you now?" Jill asked.

"Change the TV channel to 7," Ms. Zabransky said flatly.

Jill changed the channel and said, "It's hard when you need someone else to do something like change the TV channel."

After a pause Ms. Zabransky said, "Yeah."

"Do you need anything else before I go?" Jill asked.

"I used to be able to do 10 different things for 10 different people at the same time," Ms. Zabransky muttered. "Now I can't even change the damned TV channel."

"Being able to do things for yourself and others is important to you. You regret that you can't do that the way you used to," Jill added.

"Yeah . . . never mind," Ms. Zabransky responded.

"Can I sit with you for a minute before I go?" Jill asked.

"No, I'm all right," answered Ms. Zabransky.

"Okay. See you later," Jill said as she left.

It can be difficult to use active listening skills. Sometimes residents communicate in hostile ways that can be hard on caregivers. It is good to keep in mind that a resident who is behaving in a hostile way is not, at that moment, able to contain angry feelings. Those feelings come out in behaviors such as hurling insults, shouting, or using strong language. In such cases, it is important to make every effort to stay calm and contain our own angry or defensive reactions. It is natural to feel anger, confusion, or even fear while being verbally attacked. However, showing hostility in response to a patient's display of hostility is likely to create a negative cycle of increasingly difficult behavior. Acting defensively by insisting that we did nothing wrong while the resident is insisting that we did usually creates a negative cycle, too.

Once we react out of anger over being attacked, we may counterattack. We may feel justified in telling off a resident by saying things such as, "Just who do you think you are?! You can't talk to me that way! All you wanted was the channel changed! If you talk to me that way again you'll *really* wait when you push that call button!"

If a resident does "behave" in response to such a reaction from us, it is likely out of intimidation. Intimidation is not a good way of promoting optimally positive behavior and good mental or physical health, whereas positive interactions and relationships are. Intimidation or negative consequences such as being given the cold shoulder, being avoided, or having privileges withheld can undermine the kind of emotionally supportive interactions and relationships that encourage positive behavior, mental health, and physical health.

Trying to explain to an upset or confused resident why we are not at fault for his or her difficulties often leads to further confusion, upset feelings, or agitated behavior. In such situations, active listening is typically more helpful than saying, "You weren't waiting that long," "I have other people I need to help, too," or "I came as soon as you pushed the call button."

Jill did not react to Ms. Zabransky by counterattacking or being defensive. She did feel angry, confused, hurt, and frightened during the interaction with Ms. Zabransky. However, she was able to contain these feelings and not act on them. Later, she thought it was interesting that Ms. Zabransky was probably unable to contain similar feelings. She guessed Ms. Zabransky's worsening physical condition, being alone most of the time, and losing so many of her abilities left Ms. Zabransky feeling angry, confused, hurt, and frightened. Jill suspected that being overwhelmed by such feelings and unable to contain them prompted the feelings to come out in Ms. Zabransky's behavior. Luckily, Jill was able to contain herself and act as a container for what Ms. Zabransky could not contain. Drawing on Jill's strength, Ms. Zabransky regained her fragile composure.

By sharing feelings, even those behind hostile behavior, residents are often less burdened by them. When residents are less burdened by such feelings, their behavior typically improves.

Mr. Callahan

At age 79, Mr. Callahan was recovering from a stroke. His recovery had progressed well, but after approximately 2 months, he still had not regained full use of his left hand and arm.

Mr. Callahan frequently complained that he was not treated well. He often insulted people—sometimes other residents but mostly staff. His family members said that he had always been this way. They said that he looked for faults in others and was never satisfied. He demanded things but was rarely happy with what he got, they reported. Although Mr. Callahan frequently argued with and insulted people, his family noted that he hated to be alone. Mr. Callahan's behavior led many people to see him as mean, nasty, and even hateful. His behavior often drew very strong reactions from other people.

One night, Don, a nursing assistant, was checking on Mr. Callahan's roommate, who could barely move because of a degenerative neurological condition. Mr. Callahan was asleep until Don started changing the roommate's soiled pajamas.

"You no good son of a b——! What the f—— are you doing now you G—d—— idiot?!" Mr. Callahan yelled.

"I know I woke you up, Mr. Callahan. I tried to be as quiet as I could," Don explained.

"You're useless! You stupid sh—!" Mr. Callahan went on.

Because of all the noise, Carmela, another nursing assistant, came in to help out. She quietly continued assisting Mr. Callahan's roommate as Don addressed Mr. Callahan.

Don stated what he thought Mr. Callahan was thinking: "It doesn't do you any good for me to come in the middle of the night and wake you up while I help your roommate."

"That jerk. All the nurses take care of him. What about me?! Nobody gives a G—d—— about what I need!" Mr. Callahan continued loudly, although no longer yelling.

"It doesn't seem like anyone cares about your needs," Don restated Mr. Callahan's apparent reason for his feelings. Don stopped what he was doing and stood, making eye contact with Mr. Callahan.

"This whole place stinks," Mr. Callahan said in a much quieter tone while Carmela, who had finished her task, left.

"I'm sorry I woke you up," Don said as he straightened the cover of Mr. Callahan's bed. Then Don left the room and Mr. Callahan remained quiet for the rest of the night.

That was great teamwork by Don and Carmela. Carmela's help gave Don the time he needed to respond to Mr. Callahan effectively, in a way that reduced the intensity of Mr. Callahan's difficult behavior. Don handled a difficult situation with a lot of skill. He used the active listening technique of restating what appeared to be the person's underlying reasons for his or her strong feelings. Don's doing this helped to limit Mr. Callahan's abusive behavior. Mr. Callahan's behavior became less intense, then ceased when Don left the room.

Don's restating what Mr. Callahan seemed to be saying showed that he was listening to Mr. Callahan. When Don stopped what he was doing and went to Mr. Callahan's bedside, he also nonverbally showed that he was listening. Even Don's leaving the room as quickly as possible was a nonverbal way of showing that he was listening; it demonstrated that Don heard Mr. Callahan's statement about how having his sleep disrupted was another example of his needs not being considered.

By the time that Don left the room, Mr. Callahan's behavior had improved. If Don had ignored Mr. Callahan, insisted that Mr. Callahan not speak to him that way, or insisted that he stop disturbing everyone else, Mr. Callahan's problem behavior probably would not have been effectively reduced. When such approaches were tried in the past, Mr. Callahan's difficult behavior escalated to the point that he was described as being totally out of control. In one such situation, he threw a pitcher of water at a staff member while screaming, "I'll kill you!"

Having Mr. Callahan speak in a pleasant, respectful way would have been an unrealistic goal. Don was satisfied with the more realistic goal of helping Mr. Callahan to speak less loudly and decreasing the number of unpleasant things Mr. Callahan said. By using active listening techniques, Don encouraged Mr. Callahan to behave in a less difficult way. In this case, the positive behavior fostered was Mr. Callahan's moving from very difficult behavior to less difficult behavior, and the situation ended with Mr. Callahan spending the remainder of the night resting quietly.

The more that staff members used active listening in response to Mr. Callahan's complaints, insults, and threats, the less loud, insulting, and threatening his behavior became. Although Mr. Callahan still displayed some challenging behaviors, they happened much less often and usually much less intensely. Difficult episodes had initially happened several times a day; eventually, however, they rarely happened more than twice per week.

Mrs. Lowenthal

Mrs. Lowenthal was 100 years old. She was almost completely blind and not strong enough to stand and walk on her own. Although her hearing was greatly impaired, hearing aids helped somewhat. Mrs. Lowenthal was an intelligent woman and had no life-threatening illnesses. She was taking a number of medications for ongoing health problems, though.

Mrs. Lowenthal seemed depressed for some time. However, she refused to try medication for depression. She also said she did not see any sense in talking to a psychologist or any other mental health professional.

Mrs. Lowenthal sometimes spoke of being tired of living. She said, at times, that she wished she would die. However, when asked if she would ever take her own life, she clearly stated that she would never do such a thing.

One day Teresa, an LPN, was giving Mrs. Lowenthal her medications. As she swallowed them Mrs. Lowenthal said, "I'll take them, but I don't see the point."

Teresa restated what Mrs. Lowenthal said: "You don't see the point of taking your medicine."

"That's right. I don't see the point. I think this is too much fuss for someone who's been around long enough," said Mrs. Lowenthal.

"You've had a long life and you think it's been long enough," Teresa summarized.

"Well," continued Mrs. Lowenthal, "I'm blind. I'm losing my hearing. I can't even go to the toilet without help."

"You've lost so much," Teresa responded.

"That's right. That's right. I'm no use to anyone. If I got the wrong medicine and I never woke up, I would be better off," Mrs. Lowenthal said.

"You feel pretty worthless and ready to die. You're very unhappy," Teresa said. After a brief pause, she asked, "How do you feel about our talking like this?"

"I think about these things all the time. And nobody wants to hear it," Mrs. Lowenthal said as she sighed very deeply. "They ask how I'm doing, but they don't want to hear it. Not really. It's too much for them. They tell me to think about the positive things or to remember the good times. Sometimes they even say, 'Oh, Mrs. Lowenthal, I can't stand to hear what is happening to you.' Nobody knows what's happening to me. Nobody wants to know because it's too overwhelming for them. They even avoid coming to see me because it's hard for them to see what being old is like. I'm a burden . . . but you'd better go, dear. I know you have other things to do."

Teresa restated what she thought Mrs. Lowenthal meant: "You think you're burdening me."

"Well, yes. But I do know you have your work to do."

Teresa took Mrs. Lowenthal's hand and gave it a gentle squeeze. "I do need to go now, but I'll see you when I come back a little later," she said.

"Thank you, dear," responded Mrs. Lowenthal.

Teresa did an excellent job. She briefly stopped delivering medications. She restated and summarized what she thought Mrs. Lowenthal was saying. She also asked the open-ended question, "How do you feel about our talking like this?" Unlike yes-or-no or either-or questions, the occasional open-ended question can help when we are using active listening. It shows the person that we are listening, that we are available and interested in hearing what he or she has to say.

Teresa's question helped her determine how their conversation was affecting Mrs. Lowenthal. Teresa had suspected that talking that way was only making

Mrs. Lowenthal feel worse. However, Teresa found out that Mrs. Lowenthal believed that no one—including Teresa—wanted to listen to her.

Teresa thought it was interesting that both she and Mrs. Lowenthal had been afraid that the other was feeling overwhelmed. Teresa acknowledged to herself that it *was* hard for her to witness the end-of-life experience that was nearly overtaking Mrs. Lowenthal. It upset Teresa to think of how desolate it must feel to be in such circumstances: failing eyesight, diminishing hearing, continually decreasing mobility, being alone most of the time, and waiting for death. It was potentially overwhelming for Teresa to be in touch with what was happening to Mrs. Lowenthal.

Empathically understanding someone else means that we feel a bit of what that person feels. Mrs. Lowenthal's experience was that no one wanted to be close enough to her to understand her in this way. When others told her to think about positive things or remember good times or said they could not stand to hear what was happening to her, she believed that they were trying to avoid being overwhelmed by her experience. It left her feeling very alone.

At the same time, Mrs. Lowenthal prompted people to leave her alone, just as she tried to get Teresa to go on with her work. In future interactions, by using active listening and tolerating the feelings that she encountered, Teresa encouraged Mrs. Lowenthal to talk more about herself, her feelings, her experience, her life, and her death. In talking this way, Mrs. Lowenthal felt less alone and depressed. Shortly before she died, Mrs. Lowenthal thanked Teresa and said that because of her, she would not feel quite so alone when she died.

Teresa's use of active listening encouraged Mrs. Lowenthal's positive behavior of talking about her thoughts and feelings; it also increased Mrs. Lowenthal's interactions with others. These positive behaviors replaced her problem behavior of isolating herself because of depression.

Mr. Deuval

Mr. Deuval, age 73, had his left leg amputated below the knee because of diabetes. Approximately 6 months later, he was diagnosed with a fast-growing cancer that had already spread throughout much of his body. He was not expected to live much longer.

Mr. Deuval seemed very depressed. His treatment involved taking antidepressant medication and having weekly visits from the unit social worker. The recreational therapist checked in with Mr. Deuval occasionally, hoping that Mr. Deuval would become more actively involved in therapeutic recreation. The chaplain also visited periodically.

One day when Mr. Deuval was alone in his room, Alma, a nursing assistant, came in to make his bed. "How are you this morning, Mr. Deuval?" she asked cheerfully. Mr. Deuval sat in his wheelchair without replying. Alma quietly finished the bed, then said, "It's a beautiful day." Mr. Deuval still said nothing. Alma commented, "I guess you don't feel much like talking now—or maybe it is too hard for you to talk right now." When she was done straightening up the room, she said, "You seem to be feeling very down. Could I sit with you for just a minute before I leave?" Mr. Deuval did not answer. He looked at her and then looked away. "I'll sit for just a minute," Alma said, "If you want me to go, just say so." She sat in a chair and looked out the window for a minute. Then she got up and said good-bye. As she was walking out the door, Mr. Deuval said, "Thank you."

"You're very welcome, Mr. Deuval," Alma responded.

In this example, Alma "listened" to Mr. Deuval's nonverbal communication. She accepted what he was feeling when she did not try to convince him to talk or to "snap out of it." She made it clear that she was listening to Mr. Deuval when she took a minute to just sit with him. Alma also showed that she was paying attention when she stated what she thought his nonverbal communication might mean: "I guess you don't feel much like talking now—or maybe it is too hard for you to talk right now." Naming Mr. Deuval's feeling ("You seem to be feeling very down") was another way that Alma showed she was paying attention to Mr. Deuval.

Alma did not make suggestions, give advice, reassure, or offer a different way of looking at things. This was a good approach. After all, Mr. Deuval's not speaking made it hard to know what to suggest, advise, reassure, or offer.

Overall, Alma did a very good job. She respected and tolerated Mr. Deuval's feelings. Doing this, she took a step toward helping him be less isolated in his despair. Alma helped Mr. Deuval decrease his withdrawn behavior, even if only slightly.

Active listening calls for accepting what a person is expressing. People typically feel that they are being accepted when they are listened to in this way. They often say that it makes them feel respected, as though they matter or have worth. What they think and feel, what they experience as who they are, is seen, accepted, or tolerated as we listen empathetically. Being listened to in this way encourages positive behavior. It also may soothe confused, angry, agitated, or depressed residents. Our ability to engage in interactions with such individuals depends largely on our ability to tolerate the feelings that we have as we deal with the residents' emotions. That means working to tolerate the feelings, not avoiding them, denying them, acting them out, or being overwhelmed by them. For example, we may feel anger in response to a resident who angrily shouts, criticizes, blames, or threatens. Yet, if we are too uncomfortable to acknowledge our own anger to ourselves, are too frightened by the strength of our reaction, or respond in a hostile counterattack, we will not react with empathy. In turn, we might lose an opportunity to affect the resident positively or decrease problem behavior.

We can feel frightened, overwhelmed, stressed, helpless, hopeless, useless, and worthless in our work with nursing home residents—with their problem behaviors, their illnesses, the circumstances of their lives, or the circumstances of their deaths. It can be difficult to contain these feelings and remain tolerant and accepting of the residents, who frequently have similar feelings. Yet, how well we deal with these feelings will influence how effectively we provide the kind of experiences in which nursing home residents feel listened to, tolerated, accepted, and respected in ways that promote positive behavior. Try completing Exercise 2.1 to add to your personal understanding of the ideas presented up to this point in the chapter.

Exercise 2.1

Think about an episode in which a resident behaved in a way that was problematic. (A problem behavior hurts the person or someone else physically or emotionally.) If you can not think of an episode in which a nursing home resident engaged in a problem behavior, think of one in which someone else did.

Briefly describe what that person was saying and how that person was behaving:

Briefly describe the following:

1. How you used, or could have used, your body language to show the person that you were listening

2. How you restated, or could have restated, the meaning of the person's words or actions in your own words

3. How you named, or could have named, the emotion that the person was experiencing

4. How you restated, or could have restated, what the person believed were the reasons for his or her feelings

ALLOWING CHOICES

Much of a nursing home resident's experience makes it difficult for him or her to keep feeling like a capable, worthwhile individual. By the time that a person comes to a nursing home, he or she has already probably lost much, such as a home and important relationships with his or her spouse, children, friends, co-workers, and colleagues. Having to increasingly rely on others as one's senses and physical and cognitive abilities decline can cause a horrifying loss of self, of who one is or is supposed to be.

The things we do that support and acknowledge a resident's individuality or autonomy, even as these decrease, can help the person cope with the sometimes overwhelming despair and fear about this sense of disintegration. As we support the resident's sense of being someone of worth, we encourage positive behaviors that replace the negative ones prompted by the fear, angry revolt, and despair the person might feel because of what is happening at this stage of his or her life.

One technique for supporting a resident's sense of worth and autonomy is allowing him or her to make choices. When we allow a resident to routinely make choices, we show that we recognize the importance of his or her having a say in what is happening. We are providing more of the support that encourages positive behaviors. Encouraging and supporting as much decision making as possible is in turn a way of encouraging and supporting independent functioning. Encouraging and supporting decision making fosters cooperation with the care that is necessary for optimal health. People tend to be more independently involved in and cooperative with things in which they have some say. It is important that we support and encourage everyday decision making about things that do not place the resident or others at immediate risk of harm and to the degree that an individual is interested and capable.

Framing Choices

Making a choice is an independent act that can become increasingly important when illness or other circumstances make other independent acts, such as routine activities of daily living, impossible. We can often encourage a resident's making choices by framing them as open-ended questions, those that are not either-or or yes-or-no questions. These questions are good to use while assisting residents with activities of daily living, such as dressing, bathing, or eating. For example, "What time would you like to go to bed tonight?" is an open-ended question. Such questions are most helpful with residents who are interested in and capable of making these decisions. If the resident refuses to make a decision when given this kind of choice, consider using active listening before asking the question again.

Open-ended questions can be helpful in many situations. For instance, they may foster a sense of independence in residents who are facing numerous treatment options for health or rehabilitation issues. Such questions can be helpful with cooperative residents and those whose thinking has not been significantly impaired by illness. They can be used during therapeutic recreation and physical therapy sessions in which there are activities or exercises from which to choose.

Limited-choice questions can be used to encourage a resident's active involvement in decision making, too. These are "yes-or-no" questions (e.g., "Would you like to get out of bed now?) or "either-or" questions (e.g., "Would you like to get out of bed now or when I come back in 20 minutes?"). These questions, like open-ended questions, can be used with residents who are interested in and able to make decisions or cooperate. For most residents who are able and willing to make decisions and who cooperate with needed care, however, it is usually better to use open-ended questions more than limited-choice questions.

Limited-choice questions can be particularly helpful for residents who are prone to bad moods or easily confused and, as such, are not interested in or capable of making decisions or cooperating. Yes-or-no questions often are not as helpful as either-or questions. By offering limited choices, we let the resident know what our goal or expectation is (e.g., that we will help the resident out of bed) in a way that may help reduce confusion and confrontation. It allows a choice within limits —something that can be helpful in engaging the cooperation of a resident who is inclined to resist cooperating or is easily confused by too many options.

Whether we use open-ended questions or limited-choice questions, it is important to ask only one question at a time and wait for an answer before asking another question. This can show that we are interested and want to understand the resident's wishes.

When working with a new resident or one whose ability or inclination to make decisions or cooperate has improved (e.g., medical conditions—such as delirium— are effectively addressed, psychotic symptoms improve, agitation decreases, or overwhelming stress has been reduced), it is good to start with open-ended questions to see how the person reacts to them. These questions could be posed during routine activities of daily living, recreational activities, or physical therapy. If the resident resists cooperating or shows signs of confusion or agitation, try limited-choice questions instead.

If using the limited-choice questions does not reduce the confusion or agitation or does not engage the resident's cooperation, it may be best to take a break from asking questions. This could be a good time to try active listening again. Once the agitation or confusion seems sufficiently reduced, it may be good to try another limited-choice question. However, if a resident's agitated or confused behavior does not decrease as you use active listening and offer choices, leave the resident alone until the behavior stops (as long as doing so would not pose immediate risk to either the resident or anyone else). At such times, it can be helpful to ask a co-worker to take over—especially one who works well with difficult situations— if immediate care is necessary.

Once the resident has calmed down, it may be helpful to try another technique if using both types of questions does not work. This technique can also help if a resident has not behaved in a confused or agitated way but still does not cooperate with necessary care. It entails giving simple step-by-step explanations of what you are doing or what you need the resident to do. For example, while holding the resident's shirt you might say, "I'll help you put on your shirt. Here we go." Then, while holding the resident's wrist and guiding his or her arm, you might say,

"Now, put this arm through this sleeve." When using this technique, it is important to praise the resident's effort and participation to reassure and encourage him or her. Display 2.2 summarizes the approach of allowing choices to encourage positive behavior; Exercise 2.2 is provided to help emphasize the concepts covered in this section.

USING PRAISE, COMPLIMENTS, AND ACKNOWLEDGMENT

Giving praise and compliments shows appreciation. It sends the message that what is praised has worth and value. When we praise a resident's actions, we acknowledge that person's individual ability, effort, or contribution. Giving genuine praise is a way of providing positive attention and can encourage the behavior that is praised. When people regularly receive such praise, compliments, or acknowledgment, they tend to feel valued and appreciated for who they are. They often feel that what is good about them is seen, accepted, or supported. They frequently have warm, affectionate, loving feelings for those by whom they feel held in positive regard.

It is important to praise, compliment, and acknowledge residents regularly for their positive behaviors or efforts, even for things that they are "just supposed to do." Praise, compliments, and acknowledgment are good reinforcers of behavior. In fact, such social reinforcers are typically the best kinds.

Mr. Weldon

During a particularly hectic time for the staff, Mr. Weldon, a resident, sat quietly nearby waiting for help calling his daughter. When a staff member was able to help Mr. Weldon, she said, "Mr. Weldon, it was good of you to sit quietly while we were all so busy. It was such a calming influence. Thank you for waiting." This acknowledgment was especially important because Mr. Weldon frequently has difficulty being patient.

Mrs. Hamadi

Praising effort, and not just successful task completion, can encourage the positive behavior of continued effort.

Mrs. Hamadi had been refusing for several days to do any of the range of motion exercises that her physical therapist, Jenna, recommended for rehabilitation after a stroke. When Mrs. Hamadi finally let Jenna bend and stretch her paralyzed arm, Jenna said, "Good work, Mrs. Hamadi. Good work with your exercises today." Mrs. Hamadi still refused to allow Jenna to work the affected leg. Jenna said, "Why don't we just give it a little try," as she reached for Mrs. Hamadi's leg. Mrs. Hamadi screamed until Jenna stepped back. Jenna said, "I guess you want me to listen to you when you say no the first time. I'm sorry for having gone too far. Well, you did some good work today on your arm. I'm glad we were able to work on that together."

Allowing Choices

Allow nursing home residents to make choices to encourage positive behavior. It is important to support decision making when residents are interested and capable of doing this.

Open-ended questions can help encourage capable and interested residents to make decisions regarding their treatment, including the care and assistance they receive with activities of daily living such as bathing, eating, and dressing. Unlike "either-or" and "yes-or-no" questions, open-ended questions do not have set answers.

Examples of open-ended questions

- "When would you like to get out of bed today?"
- "When would you like to take your shower?"
- "What would you like to wear today?"
- "What time would you like to go to bed tonight?"

Limited-choice questions can help encourage residents who are less capable or interested in cooperating with necessary care because of confusion or bad moods. They can also be helpful when the choices you can offer are limited. These questions can often encourage positive, cooperative behaviors. "Yes-and-no" and "either-or" questions are types of limited-choice questions.

Examples of limited-choice questions

- "May I help you with your lunch tray?"
- "Would you like me to help you out of bed now or when I can come back in 30 minutes?"
- "Would you like to take your shower this morning, or will you take it tomorrow?"
- "Which would you like to wear, the blue shirt or the green shirt?"
- "You can be the first or the third person I help to bed tonight. Which would you prefer?"

Very confused or overly stressed residents might not make decisions well or may not understand the choices given to them. They may get agitated when given more choices than they can deal with, so it can be helpful to give simple step-by-step explanations of what you are doing and what you need the resident to do. For example, you might say, "I'll help you put on your shirt. Here we go. Now, put this arm through this sleeve. Very good." It is important to praise the resident's effort and participation to reassure and encourage the resident.

Caring for People with Challenging Behaviors: Essential Skills and Successful Strategies in Long-Term Care
© 2005 Stephen Weber Long. Published by Health Professions Press, Inc. (http://www.healthpropress.com).
All rights reserved.

Exercise 2.2

Think of a time when you were providing care, therapy, or other services to a nursing home resident. If you cannot think of such an example, think of a time you were working on something with another person.

Briefly describe what the two of you were doing.

Briefly describe the following:

1. How you gave, or could have given, that person choices by using open-ended questions

2. How you gave, or could have given, choices by using limited-choice questions

3. How you gave, or could have given, step-by-step explanations of what you were doing

Jenna used praise well. She did not stay focused on what Mrs. Hamadi did not do or mention the screaming. Instead, Jenna praised Mrs. Hamadi's positive behavior. Jenna also used active listening by restating what she thought Mrs. Hamadi meant by her scream. Over the next few weeks, Mrs. Hamadi tolerated more bending and stretching of her arm and even began doing it on her own. Jenna then asked Mrs. Hamadi which of the recommended leg exercises she wanted to do. Mrs. Hamadi requested the one in which Jenna would just lift Mrs. Hamadi's extended leg slightly as she lay on the exercise table. Jenna praised Mrs. Hamadi's positive behavior of selecting an exercise by saying, "Good choice," and then asked "Would you like to start with that exercise or do it at the end of our session?" Mrs. Hamadi said that she would prefer to do it at the end of the session. "Great," Jenna replied, positively affirming Mrs. Hamadi's choice. Mrs. Hamadi did the exercise at the end of the session, and Jenna acknowledged this participation with a smile, a hug, and the remark, "Great work on that leg."

Mrs. Swensen

Mrs. Swensen, who was very frail and weak, asked her nursing assistant, Kara, for help getting into bed. Kara was on her way to help the resident in the room next to Mrs. Swensen's, so she told Mrs. Swensen that she would help her in approximately 15 minutes. The wait turned out to be only 10 minutes. Although Mrs. Swensen complained that she had been kept waiting, Kara said, "It's annoying to be kept waiting. Even though it is annoying, you did it, and it was a help to me that you were able to wait. Thank you." Kara complimented Mrs. Swensen on her helpful behavior of waiting. Kara also used active listening by naming Mrs. Swensen's apparent feeling (annoyance). Also, she restated what she thought Mrs. Swensen gave as the cause of her annoyance—waiting.

Using praise and other techniques, such as active listening, encourages positive behavior. It can also help a resident value his or her relationship with you. A valued relationship, in turn, can encourage a wide range of positive behaviors. For instance, after Kara thanked Mrs. Swensen for waiting, Mrs. Swensen responded, "Oh, that's okay." Kara's skillful, empathic interaction with Mrs. Swensen continued as Kara smiled and offered Mrs. Swensen a choice about which nightgown to wear to bed.

In addition to praise, other expressions of acknowledgment promote positive behaviors and a sense of personal worth in residents. These are simple things such as regularly saying "Hello," "Good-bye," and "Thank you." Acknowledgment can be conveyed by nonverbal means as well, such as smiling, nodding in affirmation, winking, or giving a thumbs-up sign. Patting a resident on the back, shoulder, or arm; putting your arm around a resident's shoulders; or hugging a resident also can be warm expressions of acknowledgment. Most nursing home residents are likely to welcome and benefit from physical contact of this type; however, be sure to respect the wishes of those who are uncomfortable with this kind of touching. Display 2.3 offers an overview of this section on using praise, compliments, and acknowledgment; Exercise 2.3 presents personal applications for this section's content.

Using Praise, Compliments, and Acknowledgment

Praising or complimenting nursing home residents' specific behaviors encourages and reinforces those behaviors. This makes those behaviors more likely to happen again.

Praising, complimenting, and acknowledging positive behaviors are social reinforcers of behavior. Social reinforcers are typically the best kind of reinforcers.

Reinforcing positive behaviors is the best way of reducing problem behaviors.

Remember to make positive comments that praise, compliment, and acknowledge positive things that residents do (particularly residents who commonly engage in challenging behavior). Make at least four positive comments for every one negative comment (e.g., about something that a resident should stop doing).

In addition to praise and compliments, use nonverbal reinforcers, such as the following:

Smiles	Thumbs-up signs
Nods of approval or acknowledgment	Pats on the back
Hugs	Winks

Remember to praise, compliment, and acknowledge residents' efforts and partial successes at positive, helpful, appropriate, independent, or cooperative behaviors. This can be especially important with residents who frequently behave in difficult ways.

Be on the lookout for residents behaving in positive ways, and praise, compliment, or acknowledge what they are doing often.

Exercise 2.3

Think of a time when you were interacting with a nursing home resident, perhaps while providing care, therapy, or assistance or while just passing him or her in the hall. If you cannot think of an example that involved a nursing home resident, choose an interaction you had with someone else.

Briefly describe the interaction.

Briefly describe the following:

1. Positive efforts the other person made during the interaction or at other times

2. Anything the person did during the interaction or at other times that was at least not negative

3. How you praised, complimented, or acknowledged — or could have praised, complimented, or acknowledged — those positive or neutral things (neutral behaviors can be considered progress toward more positive behaviors)

Caring for People with Challenging Behaviors: Essential Skills and Successful Strategies in Long-Term Care
© 2005 Stephen Weber Long. Published by Health Professions Press, Inc. (http://www.healthpropress.com).
All rights reserved.

THINGS TO AVOID WHEN TRYING
TO ENCOURAGE POSITIVE BEHAVIOR

This chapter has presented ways to encourage residents' positive behavior. Some examples have touched on things to avoid in dealing with residents. When trying to encourage positive behavior, it is best to avoid things such as showing annoyance, frustration, or anger at a resident who is behaving in a difficult way. It is also important to avoid getting into power struggles with a resident while trying to get him or her to stop a problem behavior. Furthermore, avoid nagging, arguing, repeatedly demanding that a resident do something (or stop doing something), making threats, negative teasing (i.e., laughing at the resident by making him or her the butt of jokes), using sarcasm, scolding, or giving the resident "a dose of one's own medicine" (e.g., threatening a resident who makes threats, shouting at a resident who shouts, insulting a resident who has insulted you); see Display 2.4 for additional examples of things to avoid. These actions do not usually bring the best results. In fact, they often trigger and reinforce some of the problem behaviors. Instead, it is best to encourage positive behavior by using techniques such as active listening; providing choices; and using praise, compliments, and acknowledgment.

USING RELAXATION TECHNIQUES

Chapter 1 mentioned the importance of managing our overall stress level. Keeping our overall level of stress down can help us address the challenging behaviors of residents. If we are not overstressed when we are confronted by a stressful situation, we are more likely to deal with that situation effectively.

A very good way of reducing stress is to spend some time each day relaxing, clearing our minds of stressful thoughts and releasing tension from our bodies. Setting aside 10–20 minutes per day to practice the following relaxation techniques can help significantly reduce your stress level. With regular practice, many people find these methods easy, effective, and enjoyable.

First, choose a comfortable place where you will not be disturbed for 10–20 minutes. It is good to pick a regular time and place for practicing relaxation exercises, particularly when you are learning to use them.

Get into a comfortable position. Sitting or lying down is fine, but you may risk falling asleep if you choose to lie down. Sleeping may sometimes help with stress, but the goal of these techniques is triggering and maintaining your body's ability to relax while you are awake. Staying awake, although deeply relaxed, takes practice—practice you will not get if you fall asleep.

Do not use an alarm clock to indicate the end of your session. When you think the time is up, open your eyes and check the clock or your watch. End the session by slowly rousing yourself, moving your arms and legs as you get ready to go on with your day.

If any of the relaxation techniques in this chapter or other chapters will cause you pain or discomfort, talk with your health care professional. It may be possible

Things to Avoid When Trying to Encourage Positive Behavior

When trying to help a nursing home resident reduce, eliminate, or prevent a problem behavior, it is important to avoid the following:

- Nagging

- Arguing

- Repeatedly demanding that the resident do (or not do) something

- Making threats (e.g., "If you don't stop asking me for a cigarette, you won't get one" or "If you don't stop talking to me that way, you won't get out of bed")

- Giving the resident a "dose of his or her own medicine" (e.g., insulting a resident who insults you)

- Withholding privileges

- Ignoring the resident

- Scolding or reprimanding

- Using punishment

- Defensively insisting that things are not the way the resident sees them

- Laughing at the resident by making him or her the butt of jokes

- Engaging in power struggles

- Showing annoyance, frustration, or anger

These actions are not typically effective responses to problem behavior. Rather, they often trigger or reinforce problem behavior.

Caring for People with Challenging Behaviors: Essential Skills and Successful Strategies in Long-Term Care

to modify these techniques so you can use them, or you may be advised to avoid certain techniques.

Progressive Muscle Relaxation

As you are sitting or lying comfortably, close your eyes. Take three deep breaths. Breathe in slowly, each time silently counting up to 5 as you do. Breathe out slowly, each time silently counting up to 10 as you do. Do not count too fast when you breathe in or out. Some people find that counting "one-one thousand, two-one thousand, three-one thousand" and so on helps them count at a good pace.

After breathing out your third deep breath, focus your attention on the muscles of your legs. Tense your leg muscles and hold the tension as you silently count to 5. Again, do not count too fast. Then, gradually release the tension in your legs as you count to 10. Allow the muscles of your legs to slacken. Notice how your legs feel comfortably heavier as they become relaxed.

Now focus on the muscles of your arms. Close your hands into fists. As you tighten your fists, tighten the muscles of your arms. Hold that tension to the count of 5 before gradually releasing it as you count to 10. Feel how your arms seem to become comfortably heavy as the muscles become increasingly relaxed.

Next, tense your abdominal muscles. Hold the tension to the count of 5. Then, as you gradually relax those muscles, count to 10 silently. Feel your abdominal muscles, and the back muscles that tightened when you tensed your abdomen, become limp.

Now, bring your attention to your neck, shoulders, and upper back. Tilt your head back, pull your shoulders up and back, and hold the tension to the count of 5. Release that tension as you slowly count to 10. Notice how these muscles feel as they loosen and become comfortably relaxed as you count.

Consider your face muscles next. Tense these by shutting your eyes more tightly, clenching your teeth, and tightly pursing your lips—all at the same time. Count to 5 as you hold the tension in your facial muscles, then count to 10 as you release the tension.

Continue allowing tension to be released from any part of your body when you notice it. If you feel tension in your lower back, let it go. If you feel tension in your shoulders, neck, or jaw, let it go. Each time you exhale, let go of a little more tension. As you do this, you may feel the weight of your body as it is supported by the surface on which you are sitting or lying down (e.g., your chair, bed, or couch). Notice the feelings associated with being relaxed, and with each breath, allow yourself to become more deeply relaxed.

Sometimes as people become deeply relaxed, a set of muscles will jerk on its own. This is usually just a sign of being very, very relaxed. If it happens to you, see it as an indication of how well you are letting tension leave your body.

Some people begin to feel anxious as they practice relaxation techniques. They report feeling that they are losing control. If this happens, it may be helpful to show yourself that the process of relaxing is really under your control. At any time during your practice, you can open your eyes and then close them again to

Progressive Muscle Relaxation

Spending 10–20 minutes per day clearing your mind and releasing tension from your body is an excellent method of managing the negative effects of stress on your mental and physical health and on your relationships with others. The following steps for progressive muscle relaxation can help. *Do not do this or any other relaxation technique that causes you discomfort or pain; consult your health care professional for advice.*

1. **Pick a comfortable place** where you will not be disturbed for 10–20 minutes. Sit or lie down. Close your eyes.

2. **Take three slow, deep breaths.** As you breathe in, slowly and silently count to 5 (e.g., "one one-thousand, two one-thousand. . . ."). Then, slowly count to 10 as you exhale. For the rest of this exercise, breathe normally and naturally.

3. **Tense your leg muscles.** Then, slowly release the tension. You can do this step by pushing down with your legs to tense the muscles. Hold the tension until you do a slow, silent count to 5. Release the tension as you slowly count to 10.

4. **Tense and relax your arm muscles.** First, close your hands into fists. Tighten your fists. Push down with your arms. Feel the tension and hold it, counting slowly to 5. Then, release the tension gradually as you count to 10.

5. **Focus on your abdominal muscles.** Tighten those muscles. Hold the tension and count to 5. Release the tension to the count of 10.

6. **Tense the muscles of your neck, shoulders, and upper back.** Then, gradually release the tension. You can do this step by tilting your head back while pulling your shoulders up and back. Hold the tension to the count of 5. Release the tension while counting to 10.

7. **Focus on your face muscles.** Tense these muscles by shutting your eyes more tightly, clenching your teeth, and tightly pursing your lips — all at the same time. Hold the tension to the count of 5. Then, release the tension gradually as you count to 10.

After going through these seven steps, continue allowing tension to leave any muscles that remain tight. Each time you exhale, let go of more tension and allow yourself to feel more relaxed.

(continued)

Display 2.5 *(continued)*

It is best not to fall asleep while you are practicing relaxation exercises. The goal is to become more skilled at triggering and maintaining your body's ability to relax while you are awake.

Do not use an alarm clock to indicate the end of your session. When you think the time is up, open your eyes and check. If the time is not up, close your eyes and continue your practice.

Sometimes people feel nervous, as though they are losing control, while becoming deeply relaxed. If this happens, open your eyes to show yourself that the process of relaxation is under your control. Then, gradually allow yourself to continue becoming more skillful at controlling your body's ability to become deeply relaxed.

Caring for People with Challenging Behaviors: Essential Skills and Successful Strategies in Long-Term Care

continue becoming as relaxed as you prefer. You can also choose to end your relaxation session at any time. Making these choices as you practice the relaxation techniques allows you to gradually increase the benefits you receive. See Display 2.5 for a quick guide to progressive muscle relaxation.

SUMMARY

Chapter 2 dealt with effective approaches to encouraging positive behavior among nursing home residents. The chapter made five main points regarding behavior. First, encouraging, triggering, and reinforcing positive behavior are the best ways to reduce or eliminate difficult behavior. The more often a person is involved in doing positive things, the less likely it is that he or she will behave in challenging ways.

Second, promoting, encouraging, and reinforcing positive behavior are more effective in reducing challenging behavior than reprimanding, arguing, withholding privileges, or doing anything that the resident would experience as punishment. Punishment is not the most effective way to promote positive behavior.

Third, three effective approaches to encouraging positive behavior are using active listening; allowing choices; and using praise, compliments, and acknowledgment. Active listening encourages the positive behavior of expressing thoughts and feelings in words and other positive behaviors. Allowing choices encourages both independence and cooperation. Using praise, compliments, and acknowledgment lets residents know that they do things that are of worth and reinforces those positive behaviors.

Fourth, approaches for fostering positive behavior can help a resident value his or her relationship with you. Valued relationships can promote a wide range of positive behaviors.

Fifth, avoid nagging, arguing, making repeated demands, making threats, or retaliating against a resident who behaves in difficult ways. Generally, avoid negative responses to residents' challenging behaviors. Keep in mind that it is important to use positive approaches and avoid negative responses to problem behavior with all nursing home residents but especially those who most often behave in difficult ways.

Chapter 2 also continued the theme of stress management's role in effectively addressing difficult situations with residents. In particular, the chapter described the technique of progressive muscle relaxation.

Finding Solutions to Difficult Behavior

Chapter 2 looked at how our actions can encourage, trigger, or reinforce nursing home residents' positive behavior. This fact is related to an important point about behavior: Every behavior—good or bad—happens for a reason.

Chapter 3 explores methods of understanding behavior that can help us, and residents, find solutions to difficult behavior. It describes the "ABCs of Behavior" and cooperative problem solving. In addition, the chapter describes "holding on," a method to help us contain our reactions to residents' difficult behaviors. Chapter 3 also explains the use of imagery to deal with stress.

THE IMPORTANCE OF UNDERSTANDING PROBLEM BEHAVIORS

Sometimes nursing home staff make statements such as, "She hits people for no reason" or "His agitated behavior is unpredictable." These statements can be right in a certain sense if we mean, for example, that the hitting is done without what is considered acceptable justification or that the agitated behavior is difficult to understand well enough to predict when it is likely to happen.

As discussed in Chapter 2, however, using active listening often can help us find which things prompt or reinforce a resident's challenging behaviors. By using active listening effectively, we can get in touch with the thoughts and feelings that contribute to the resident's behavior. Being prepared to tolerate the thoughts and feelings stirred up in us as we do this is an important part of learning why a resident behaves in difficult ways. Understanding the resident's thoughts and feelings in this way can help us to adjust the resident's environment in ways that he or she is not able to or in ways that convey our respect and concern. We can adjust external influences contributing to the distress that typically underlie and fuel the resident's difficult behavior.

The things that we adjust can be thought of as triggers and reinforcers of behavior. For example, we might discover that for one resident, being told not to talk in a despairing manner triggers his or her withdrawal into isolation and depression. We may also discover that as a consequence of the resident's withdrawal, others do not talk to or interact much with him or her, reinforcing this person's isolation, despair, and withdrawal. In such a case, we can begin to adjust either the trigger that comes before the withdrawing behavior or the reinforcing consequence that follows it. We could also adjust both the trigger and the reinforcing consequence. For example, we might avoid saying, "Don't talk that way," and use active listening instead, changing what happens before the individual withdraws into isolation (i.e., changing the behavior's triggering antecedent). Then we might also change the reinforcing consequence of the resident's withdrawn behavior, perhaps by interacting with the resident in at least small ways, to the level that he or she can tolerate. Active listening can be used at these times, too.

THE ABCs OF BEHAVIOR AND INTERPERSONAL INTERACTION

As noted, the term *behavioral trigger* denotes something that came before a behavior—that is, an antecedent of the behavior. When we speak about what happens in response to the behavior, we are talking about a consequence of the behavior. A consequence may contribute to whether a behavior continues or gets stronger. It can reinforce the behavior. Reinforcing consequences come after the behavior.

The ABCs of Behavior concept can help us understand residents' behavior: There is at least one **A**ntecedent to each **B**ehavior, and a behavior that continues or gets stronger has at least one reinforcing **C**onsequence. The ABCs of Behavior method, like active listening, is a useful tool for understanding some of the causes of behavior.

It is important to remember that no behavior is likely to have *only* internal or *only* external antecedents or consequences. We cannot directly change past events that have led to habits of behavior or lifelong ways of looking at things. Our ability to eliminate or modify a person's predispositions is limited. There are some things about the internal processes of mental and physical illnesses that we may not easily or quickly influence—and others that we may not be able to influence at all.

However, we can often have a direct, immediate influence on many of the external antecedents or consequences of a resident's behavior. We do this by first determining which external antecedents may have triggered the behavior and determining which external consequences may have reinforced the behavior. The ABCs of Behavior approach looks at the process—or the context—in which a behavior happens. By reviewing this process, we often find previously unknown factors that have been influencing how the resident behaves. In many cases, if we become more aware of this process, we will be able to choose to adjust it in ways that have a positive effect on the individual's behavior.

It is helpful to remember that what we do in our interactions with residents is the most important source of behavioral reinforcement. In addition, our behavior may be a major source of triggering antecedents and reinforcing consequences. See Display 3.1 for a review of this topic.

Antecedents and Consequences

Mrs. Nicolls Mrs. Nicolls was 69 years old. She had difficulty walking and felt dizzy whenever she stood, so she used a wheelchair.

Felicity, a nursing assistant, was new to the nursing home. She had never worked with Mrs. Nicolls before, but others described Mrs. Nicolls as "difficult." She heard that Mrs. Nicolls did not cooperate when she was being helped. It was also said that Mrs. Nicolls always accused people of taking her things, argued about everything, and remembered only what she wanted to remember. In addition, staff said that Mrs. Nicolls always hit others. Whenever she was told that she should not hit others, however, Mrs. Nicolls said she never hit a soul. Finally, Mrs. Nicolls, who was Caucasian, was also described as a racist.

Felicity, who was an African American, was pleasantly surprised that Mrs. Nicolls was not very fussy with her. However, she was unsettled to see Mrs. Nicolls hit others. This occurred each day after Mrs. Nicolls had finished lunch, just outside the dining room.

Because Mrs. Nicolls and many other residents who used wheelchairs moved slowly, there was usually a "traffic jam" of wheelchairs outside the dining room door. The residents bumped into each other, trying to make their way down that crowded section of hallway. Very confused or frail residents would just sit in the way of the others.

Each day, Mrs. Nicolls was one of the first to leave the dining room, but she ended up in the middle of the traffic jam as others caught up to and bumped into her. After being bumped a few times, Mrs. Nicolls would curse and punch the next person who bumped her. The more she got bumped, the louder she would curse and the more she would hit. Some other residents cursed back at her, told her to stop, and even threatened to hit her back. Mrs. Nicolls only got more agitated, though—yelling and hitting even more. At these times, she kept calling another resident, who was African American, a "f——— n———."

When staff told Mrs. Nicolls that her behavior was inappropriate, she just kept hitting other residents and yelling. The cursing and hitting only stopped when a staff member took Mrs. Nicolls out of the situation.

In a situation such as the one involving Mrs. Nicolls, we can look for the antecedents and consequences that trigger and reinforce a problem behavior. Felicity decided to use the ABCs of Behavior to determine what was triggering and reinforcing Mrs. Nicolls' agitated, hostile behavior. Felicity believed that the "A"—the antecedent—of the behavior was the overcrowded section of the hallway. This appeared to trigger the "B"—the behavior—of yelling curses and racist insults and

The ABCs of Behavior

When dealing with difficult behavior, it can be helpful to remember the ABCs of Behavior:

A Every behavior—positive or negative —is triggered by something. What happens just before a behavior that triggers the behavior is an **A**ntecedent of the behavior.

B A **B**ehavior is any action. It can be good or bad, positive or negative.

C If a behavior continues or gets stronger, something that comes after the behavior— that is, some **C**onsequence of the behavior—is reinforcing the behavior.

No behavior is likely to be triggered and reinforced only by internal factors or only by external factors. We can usually have a direct, immediate effect on many external influences, thereby influencing external triggering antecedents and reinforcing consequences of a resident's problem behavior. By doing this, we can help reduce or even eliminate a problem behavior.

It is important to look at what we and others do that may trigger or reinforce residents' behavior. Other people—intentionally or not—are the most important sources of triggers and reinforcers of residents' behavior.

hitting. Felicity noticed that the "C"—the consequence—of others yelling back, threatening, or telling Mrs. Nicolls that her behavior was inappropriate apparently reinforced the problem behavior, making it continue and grow stronger. Felicity also noticed that when the consequence of Mrs. Nicolls' behavior was getting wheeled out of the overcrowded situation, the agitated behavior ended. This consequence seemed to trigger calmer behavior from Mrs. Nicolls. In identifying these apparent triggers and reinforcers, Felicity was helped by keeping in mind that the most important triggers and reinforcers happen very close in time to the behavior. Usually, they come just before and right after the behavior starts.

Changing the Antecedents that Trigger the Problem Behavior

We can use what we learn about triggers or reinforcers to manage situations—that is, to decrease the regularity or intensity of a behavior. We can try to prevent settings that trigger the behavior.

After noticing the ABCs of Mrs. Nicolls' hitting, Felicity decided to watch Mrs. Nicolls whenever she began to leave the dining room after lunch. Felicity made sure to give Mrs. Nicolls help getting beyond the area that usually got "clogged." She changed what seemed to be the "A"—the antecedent or trigger—of Mrs. Nicolls' agitated, hostile behavior. As a result, Mrs. Nicolls' hitting and agitated shouting stopped.

When Felicity was not able to work with Mrs. Nicolls, she told the person who was going to be working with Mrs. Nicolls that she had been helping Mrs. Nicolls avoid behaving in hostile, agitated ways. As other staff members increasingly followed Felicity's example, Mrs. Nicolls' challenging behavior dwindled and eventually stopped. In fact, staff members later recognized that the traffic jams were distressing to other residents, too. As a result, they ensured that there were no traffic jams in the hallways. Exercise 3.1 further emphasizes the importance of identifying triggers and reinforcers.

HOLDING ON: DEALING WITH
REACTIONS TO PROBLEM BEHAVIORS

As mentioned previously, it can be difficult to tolerate some problem behaviors. Dealing with our feelings about a resident or about his or her behavior may be far from easy. Yet, how we cope with these feelings can have a major influence on how successfully we address problem behaviors.

In Mrs. Nicolls' case, Felicity felt initially unsettled, uncertain, and confused when she saw and heard Mrs. Nicolls' agitated, hostile behavior. Her first reaction was emotional: She was angry. Then she thought, "This is not supposed to happen! This is just not supposed to happen! There is no excuse for violence or racism! Somebody should make her stop it!" Felicity thought that even though Mrs. Nicolls seemed to get along well with her, the resident's hitting, cursing, and using racial insults seemed to show that she really was violent and racist. "Here it goes again," Felicity thought, "It's always the same. Racism and abusiveness that are always

Exercise 3.1

Think about a time when a nursing home resident behaved in a way that was problematic. If you cannot think of a time when a resident behaved in such a way, think about an incident in which someone else did.

Briefly describe the behavior.

Briefly describe the following:

1. Possible external triggers for the problem behavior (Remember that the most important triggers happen very close in time to the behavior, usually just before the difficult behavior starts)

2. Possible external reinforcing consequences that might have contributed to the continuation or worsening of problem (Remember that reinforcing consequences usually happen very close in time to the behavior, usually right after the behavior starts)

3. What you did, or could have done, to change what was happening in response to the problem behavior — that is, to change the reinforcing consequences

4. What you did, or could have done, to help prevent the person's problem behavior from being triggered in the future

just under the surface come out one way or another, no matter what I do, no matter how well I do, or how helpful I am—no matter what anybody does. It will never stop." With these thoughts, her anger melted away to a feeling of hopelessness.

At this point, Felicity thought she understood what she had heard from others about Mrs. Nicolls being difficult. Mrs. Nicolls' agitated, angry behavior contributed to Felicity's initial reaction of feeling agitated and angry, too. Fortunately, Felicity was better able to *hold on* and contain these feelings; she did not act on them. Unfortunately, part of what kept Felicity from acting was a sense of hopelessness. She believed that she could do nothing. She even started to feel helpless and worthless. This only went so far, though, before Felicity began to get angry again. She found herself thinking that no one had the right to make her feel these ways, especially not Mrs. Nicolls. "I am not powerless, and I will not let anyone treat me like this," Felicity thought. She started to get fighting mad at the bumping and jostling that her sense of self always seemed to take.

Then Felicity was startled by how similar what she felt and what she wanted to do was to Mrs. Nicolls' behavior and apparent feelings when she got bumped and jostled in the hall. Felicity recognized that she was feeling empathy for Mrs. Nicolls because she understood that this was a very unpleasant experience for the woman. She saw that Mrs. Nicolls was not able to contain her feelings of anger in situations that overwhelmed her fragile abilities to cope. Felicity suspected that Mrs. Nicolls fought against feeling hopeless about her deteriorating physical and cognitive capabilities by fighting against others. By treating her African American co-resident hatefully, Felicity thought, Mrs. Nicolls was able to avoid focusing on what she hated about herself: her inability to simply get down the hallway and back to her room, her view that she was nothing more than an obstacle, a hindrance.

It seemed to Felicity that if she acted on her own angry feelings toward Mrs. Nicolls—by reprimanding her, avoiding her, or withdrawing from her—she would probably reinforce Mrs. Nicolls' negative experience of herself. She wanted to avoid doing this, as it was an experience that Felicity suspected motivated Mrs. Nicolls' problem behavior.

While thinking all of this through, Felicity noticed that she was feeling less overwhelmed by her reactions to Mrs. Nicolls. She felt compassion for Mrs. Nicolls despite her behavior and began to suspect there were ways to decrease Mrs. Nicolls' difficult behavior. In the end, using the ABCs of Behavior helped Felicity to no longer feel powerless in dealing with Mrs. Nicolls' agitated, hostile behavior. Furthermore, her work effectively dealt with a long-standing distressing problem in the nursing home. Display 3.2 provides an overview of holding on; Exercise 3.2 shows how it can be applied in your interactions with residents and others.

Ms. Oakley

Ms. Oakley was 75 years old. Her left leg was amputated below the knee due to diabetes. She usually stayed in her room talking, sometimes shouting, to someone who was not there. Her words were hard to understand; sometimes they sounded more like mumbling than actual words. When Ms. Oakley said words that were

Display 3.2

Holding On: Dealing with Reactions to Problem Behaviors

First, when you have strong feelings about something a resident did, hold on. Do not immediately react out of feelings such as anger, frustration, disgust, or hopelessness.

Second, try to see how what you feel might resemble what the resident feels.

Third, think of what behavior you would like to see from the person (e.g., helpful, cooperative, nonaggressive, considerate).

Fourth, behave in the way you would like the resident to behave, even if he or she has behaved—or is behaving—in difficult ways.

Fifth, if the resident's behavior does not become more positive, look for ways that your behavior (e.g., acting defensive, annoyed, angry, impatient, hurt, or distant) could be triggering or reinforcing the difficult behavior.

Finally, consider changing those triggers or reinforcers.

Exercise 3.2

Think of an incident in which a nursing home resident behaved in a difficult way. Think of an incident involving someone else if you cannot think of one involving a resident.

Briefly describe the difficult behavior.

What emotion was the person probably experiencing?

Was your emotion at the time similar to what the other person seemed to be feeling? If not, think of a different incident — maybe one involving a different person — in which it is easier to see the similarity between the emotions both of you were feeling.

Describe the following:

1. How you would have liked that person to behave

2. The way you behaved, or could have behaved, to exemplify the type of behavior you would have liked the other person to display

Caring for People with Challenging Behaviors: Essential Skills and Successful Strategies in Long-Term Care
© 2005 Stephen Weber Long. Published by Health Professions Press, Inc. (http://www.healthpropress.com).
All rights reserved.

understandable, she did not put them into sentences that made sense to anyone. A visit by the consulting psychiatrist, who recommended a change in Ms. Oakley's medication, lessened some of this behavior. Still, Ms. Oakley stayed to herself and said few understandable words other than "yes" or "no." Ms. Oakley only did things requested of her when she was asked to do them one at a time. Also, she did not change her clothing or wash herself, and she sometimes played with her excrement.

Miki, an LPN, was in the break room when Julio, a housekeeper, came in for some coffee. Miki looked pretty angry. Julio asked, "How's it going?"

"How's it going?! How's it going?!" she said, looking like she was trying not to explode. "She hit me! Oakley hit me! I hate this place!"

"Were you hurt?" Julio asked.

"This place is just too much!" Miki continued. "I don't come to work to be anybody's punching bag! She did it for no reason! I don't care how sick she is! She has no right to hit me!"

"You're pretty furious," Julio responded.

Miki went on, "It's always the same! You just do your best and where does it get you?! I don't have to take this abuse!"

"It's hard to go on doing your job when you get hit," Julio said.

"It is," Miki responded. "How can anyone be expected to work in a place like this? I just don't get it." Although still very angry, Miki was a bit calmer now.

"Did you report the incident?" asked Julio.

"Oh, yeah. I did the paper work and all. I was told a psychiatrist will come over to see about adjusting Oakley's medication."

"You're not hurt?" Julio asked again.

"No. Just good and fed up," Miki answered.

"Want some coffee?" Julio asked.

"No, thanks, I don't need anything else revving me up just yet," Miki said; however, she was notably less upset.

Julio and Miki sat quietly for a while.

After a few moments, Miki said, "I was walking past her room and I looked in. She was sitting on the floor with her dress up and her diaper undone. She had poop on her hand and was chuckling while she reached up and smeared it on the bedspread. You know she does that kind of thing any chance she gets. Usually, we're able to get to her often enough to keep her clean. But over the past few days because of the bad weather, people who are scheduled to work aren't getting in. And other people are away on vacation."

"Yeah, tell me about it. Everything that needs to be done can't be done quick enough. It's been impossible," responded Julio.

"It is. It really is impossible," Miki added. "So when I saw what Oakley was doing, I rushed in to stop her from making more of a mess. I yelled, 'What are you doing? Stop that! Now I have to clean all of this up, and I don't have time for this!' She looked pretty surprised. And when I grabbed her arm to make her stop, she yanked her arm out of my hand and started swinging at me. I kept telling her to stop hitting me and that her behavior wouldn't be tolerated. But she just kept trying to hit me. It was a good thing that the new charge nurse, Joan, came in. Joan said she'd take care of it. She let me go finish helping the people I was supposed to shower so I could then give out meds."

It can be difficult in the heat of a moment to hold on, contain our feelings, and use the ABCs of Behavior. Sometimes we need time to step back, calm down, and look at what happened. For Miki, taking time off in the break room was a good idea. It also helped that Julio, someone she knew and felt comfortable with, made himself available through active listening. Although it is important for us to provide residents with the kind of emotional support given through active listening, it is also important for us to provide it for each other. The more accurately we support each other, the less job stress and burnout we will feel.

Another helpful thing to do when we are calmer is to use the ABCs of Behavior method to understand what happened. This can involve writing down our observations in a way that can help us see the likely behavioral triggers and reinforcers. By doing this, we can gain a better idea of what to do to prevent triggering and reinforcing a problem behavior. The appendix contains an ABCs of Behavior Observation Form. You can photocopy it and use it to record your observations when trying to help a resident reduce or eliminate a problem behavior.

If Miki had chosen to write down the ABCs of Ms. Oakley's hitting to understand the behavior better, she might have written the following:

A Antecedent	B Behavior	C Consequence
I loudly told Ms. Oakley to stop what she was doing. I tried to stop her by holding her arm.	Ms. Oakley hit me. She repeatedly struck out at me.	I kept telling Ms. Oakley that her behavior would not be tolerated. I kept trying to restrain her arm.

Writing this down might have helped Miki see Ms. Oakley's behavior as part of an interaction. It might have given Miki a chance to think of ways to change her behavior in future interactions to have a more positive effect on Ms. Oakley's behavior. Try completing Exercise 3.3 to see how the ABCs of Behavior can apply to someone in your care.

Beyond the Interaction

As Miki and Julio's exchange made clear, things beyond the interaction between Miki and Ms. Oakley contributed to the incident. Miki was feeling overwhelmed by the amount of work she needed to do to make up for the staff members who either were away on vacation or who could not make it to work. It is hard to be at our best under such circumstances. When we are stressed by too many responsibilities, it can limit the patience needed to provide the best care to residents who have particularly difficult impairments.

Exercise 3.3

Think of a nursing home resident who engaged in a problem behavior. If you cannot think of a resident who has behaved in a difficult way, think of someone else who has. Using the following directions, fill out the ABC box for a particular incident.

First, under "B," record the problem behavior. Be specific. For example, instead of saying, "The resident was aggressive," describe the action in which the person engaged, such as, "The resident screamed that I was lazy and stupid."

Next, under "A," record what was happening to or around the resident immediately before the behavior began. Again, be specific. Instead of saying, "I was delivering care to the resident," it is more helpful to write something such as, "I told Mrs. X that I would help her out of bed in a little while, after she said that she wanted to get out of bed."

Finally, under "C," record what happened immediately in response to the person's problem behavior. Be specific. For example, rather than saying, "I reported the behavior to the charge nurse," it is better to say something such as, "I walked out of Mrs. X's room without saying anything to her."

A Antecedent	B Behavior	C Consequence

Miki struggled with feeling powerless and angry. She had less success at holding on and containing those feelings than Felicity did during her work with Mrs. Nicolls. Miki acted on her anger by trying to take control of Ms. Oakley. Fortunately, when staffing returned to adequate levels, Miki once again was able to deal effectively with Ms. Oakley.

More About the ABCs of Behavior

The ABCs of Behavior can help address a wide range of problem behaviors. A few things can make your efforts with the ABCs of Behavior successful. It is important to deal with only one or two challenging behaviors at a time. Do not try to solve all of a resident's behavior issues at the same time. To understand the ABCs of a particular behavior, stay focused on the situations in which the behavior happens. Use the ABCs of Behavior Observation Form in the appendix to record what happens to or around the resident before and after the behavior occurs. For problem behaviors that happen frequently, triggering antecedents and reinforcing consequences may be found quickly, perhaps in a few days. For problem behaviors that do not happen frequently, it could take 2 weeks or longer to find the antecedents or consequences. The following is a case example of using the ABCs of Behavior.

Mr. Youngquist   Mr. Youngquist was 70 years old. He had a stroke and was not able to use his right arm, hand, or leg. This affected his ability to perform certain activities, particularly because he was right-handed. However, psychological tests indicated that Mr. Youngquist's thinking and ability to understand others were not affected by the stroke. He often had difficulty finding the words he wanted to say, though.

Maureen, a nursing assistant, was scheduled to work with Mr. Youngquist. Whenever she helped him into his pajamas at bedtime, the same embarrassing thing happened: One way or another, he would cup her breast with his hand or grab her bottom. When she told him to stop, he said, "You know you like it." Despite her embarrassment, Maureen eventually told her supervisor, Barbara, who was also the charge nurse. When Barbara spoke with Mr. Youngquist about this behavior, he said (with some effort to speak clearly) that he never touched Maureen that way. He said that Maureen must have misunderstood his accidentally touching her while she was helping him. Barbara still responded by emphasizing that such behavior was inappropriate. It was unacceptable and would not be tolerated.

Maureen had hoped that having someone with as much authority as her supervisor talk to Mr. Youngquist would make him stop, but it did not. The next day it happened again.

Later that day, Barbara checked with Maureen to see how things were going. When Maureen said that the problem was continuing, Barbara sympathized with her. Maureen could see that the sympathy was genuine, and she understood Barbara's explanation that there were no further options for forcing Mr. Youngquist to stop other than Maureen's making formal legal charges. He could not even be discharged because his condition required skilled nursing care and his behavior would prevent any other nursing home from admitting him.

Barbara asked Maureen if the problem was so difficult that she could no longer work with Mr. Youngquist. Barbara also asked if Maureen felt abused by Mr. Youngquist or by the way the situation was being handled. Maureen said she did not feel abused by Mr. Youngquist. It would be different if she felt threatened by him or what he did, she said, but as it was, she just felt annoyed when he fondled her. She also stated that she did not feel abused by the way the situation was being handled. In fact, she appreciated Barbara's concern and support. Maureen added that the problem was not big enough for her to feel she could not work with Mr. Youngquist. She really did like him—even if he could be annoying—and felt sorry for his going through the upheaval in his life following his stroke.

Barbara asked Maureen what she thought should be done. Because Maureen had recently received some training on the ABCs of Behavior, she said that she would like to try this approach. She figured that if she could get an idea of what was triggering or reinforcing Mr. Youngquist's sexual behavior, she might be able to do something about it.

Barbara, who was familiar with the ABCs of Behavior approach, agreed that giving it a try was a good idea. She asked Maureen what she thought the ABCs were in regard to Mr. Youngquist's problem behavior. Maureen believed that his being a man had something to do with it and that maybe seeing women as sex objects triggered it, too. She guessed that Mr. Youngquist saw his behavior as a way of asserting that he was still a virile man despite all that he had been through as a result of his stroke.

Barbara said all of that might be true but that Mr. Youngquist's lifelong attitudes about women would probably not change quickly enough to help Maureen avoid being groped, and it was impossible to do anything about his being a man. Barbara pointed out, however, that changing those things was not necessary for the ABCs of Behavior approach to affect problem behavior. The ABCs of Behavior focus on what occurred just before a behavior happened to see which factors triggered the behavior. We can also look at which elements of the situation happened in response to the behavior and may reinforce it.

Barbara suggested that Maureen use five questions to get an idea of the antecedents and consequences that might trigger and reinforce Mr. Youngquist's difficult behavior. She also asked Maureen to use these questions to record the apparent ABCs of Mr. Youngquist's behavior. The five questions were as follows:

1.   When did the behavior happen—that is, at what time and on which day(s)?

2.   At what location did the problem behavior happen? Describe the setting (e.g., private, crowded, loud, quiet, busy, not much activity, well lit, dim).

3.   What was happening around or to the resident when the behavior happened?

4.   Who was interacting with the resident when the problem behavior happened?

5. What did the person interacting with the resident do just before the problem behavior started and right after it began?

See Display 3.3 for a listing of these questions in a handy photocopiable format.
    Maureen gave these answers:

1. It happened in the evenings between 8:00 P.M. and 10:00 P.M., every evening that I worked with Mr. Youngquist.

2. It only happened in Mr. Youngquist's room. It was private and quiet with the curtain drawn around his bed and the door to the room closed. No one else was in the room.

3. I was helping Mr. Youngquist to change and get into bed.

4. I was interacting with Mr. Youngquist when the problem behavior happened.

5. Mr. Youngquist grabbed my breast or bottom whenever I helped him change into his pajamas and get into bed. I told him, "Please stop touching me that way."

Maureen then used her answers to the questions to record the possible ABCs of Behavior for Mr. Youngquist:

A Antecedent	B Behavior	C Consequence
In the quiet privacy of his room, I helped Mr. Youngquist change and get into bed.	Mr. Youngquist cupped my breast or bottom with his hand.	I told him, "Please stop touching me that way."

Looking at what she wrote, Maureen could not determine anything that she did not already know. Writing the answers to the questions and filling out the observation form did not seem to help her address Mr. Youngquist's troubling behavior.

Barbara suggested that Maureen start by changing what would happen if Mr. Youngquist groped her again—changing the **C**onsequence. Maureen had been asking Mr. Youngquist to stop touching her that way. Then she would continue helping him get ready for bed. Barbara proposed that Maureen let Mr. Youngquist know there would be a different consequence if he groped her again. Barbara explained that Maureen could say something like, "Mr. Youngquist, you have a choice. While I help you get to bed, you can either keep your hands to yourself or I will stop helping you. I'll stop what I am doing with you and leave you to yourself for about 15 minutes. Then, either I or someone else will come in to try to help you. If you touch any private part of my body, I will know you have chosen for me to leave you on your own for a little while." Barbara assured Maureen that this would be perfectly fine to do as long as leaving Mr. Youngquist did not put him—or anyone else—at immediate risk of harm. Barbara pointed out that by saying

Display 3.3

Determining What Triggers and Reinforces a Resident's Problem Behavior

When we are trying to see what the triggering **A**ntecedents are to a problem **B**ehavior, and trying to see what the reinforcing **C**onsequences are for it, the following five questions can be helpful:

1. When did the behavior happen — that is, at what time and on which day(s)?

2. At what location did the problem behavior happen? Describe the setting (e.g., private, crowded, loud, quiet, busy, not much activity, well lit, dim).

3. What was happening around or to the resident when the problem behavior happened?

4. Who was interacting with the resident when the problem behavior happened?

5. What did the person interacting with the resident do just before the problem behavior started and right after it began?

this as she went into Mr. Youngquist's room, Maureen would also be changing what usually happened before his troublesome behavior—that is, changing the **A**ntecedents.

Barbara also asked Maureen to complete an ABCs of Behavior Observation Form to track Mr. Youngquist's groping behavior each day for the next week. Because the form contains space for 3 days, Maureen would need to make two copies of it to have space for each of the 5 days she would be working that week. Barbara suggested that Maureen keep using the five questions to help her complete the form. Maureen agreed to follow this suggestion.

Maureen found it hard to be assertive in her interactions with Mr. Youngquist, so she did not tell him that she would leave him alone for 15 minutes if he touched her inappropriately. At the end of the week, Maureen explained this to Barbara but noted that she did complete the ABCs of Behavior Observation Form each day. Barbara said that she hoped Maureen could work on setting limits on what she would tolerate from Mr. Youngquist, and she asked to review the observation forms with Maureen.

ABCs of Behavior Observation Form

Date: __12/6/04__   Time: __8:55 P.M.__

A Antecedent	B Behavior	C Consequence
In the quiet privacy of his room, I helped Mr. Youngquist change and get into bed.	Mr. Youngquist cupped my breast or bottom with his hand.	I told him, "Please stop touching me that way."

Date: __12/7/04__   Time: __9:35 P.M.__

A Antecedent	B Behavior	C Consequence
In the quiet privacy of his room, I helped Mr. Youngquist change and get into bed.	Mr. Youngquist cupped my breast or bottom with his hand.	I told him, "Please stop touching me that way."

Date: __12/8/04__   Time: __9:45 P.M.__

A Antecedent	B Behavior	C Consequence
In the quiet privacy of his room, I helped Mr. Youngquist change and get into bed.	Mr. Youngquist cupped my breast or bottom with his hand.	I told him, "Please stop touching me that way."

ABCs of Behavior Observation Form

Date: __12/9/04_____ Time: _____

A Antecedent	B Behavior	C Consequence
	The problem behavior did not happen today.	

Date: __12/10/04_____ Time: __9:00 P.M._____

A Antecedent	B Behavior	C Consequence
In the quiet privacy of his room, I helped Mr. Youngquist change and get into bed.	Mr. Youngquist cupped my breast or bottom with his hand.	I told him, "Please stop touching me that way."

Date: __N/A_____ Time: __N/A_____

A Antecedent	B Behavior	C Consequence
	N/A End of week	

Reviewing Observation Forms   Maureen said that except for the fourth day, the behavior happened consistently. Maureen explained that on that day Mr. Young-quist agreed to go to bed a little earlier so Maureen could help out with a resident who needed to be transferred to the hospital that evening. While Maureen was helping Mr. Youngquist, Carla, an LPN, knocked on the door, and came in with his medications. Maureen had just drawn the curtain around the bed. Carla asked if she could help out. Both Mr. Youngquist and Maureen said okay. That evening, Mr. Youngquist did not engage in the problematic behavior.

Barbara asked what Maureen thought about the conditions on the fourth night. Maureen thought that not having the usual amount of privacy might have prevented Mr. Youngquist from handling her in the way that he typically did. It looked to her as though privacy was an important triggering antecedent for Mr. Youngquist's unwelcome behavior. Barbara agreed that this hunch seemed reasonable.

Barbara suggested that she would schedule someone to assist Maureen with changing and helping Mr. Youngquist to bed each night for the next week. She thought this might show them whether having another person in the room really did help prevent his fondling Maureen. Maureen liked this idea.

Remembering to Encourage Positive Behavior   Maureen also remembered that the best way of reducing or eliminating a problem behavior is to encourage, trigger, and reinforce positive behavior. She realized that it was important for her and other staff members to encourage Mr. Youngquist's positive behaviors. Maureen decided to give Mr. Youngquist more positive attention, compliments, praise, and other social reinforcers for his efforts and successes at physical rehabilitation and for small steps toward self-care while she helped him change and get into bed. To Maureen, it seemed that the message in his behavior was that he needed to feel potent, capable of pleasing and of being the object of affection. He wanted to feel he was fully acceptable as a person in general and as a man in particular. He needed to feel valued and that his affection had meaning—even if some of his ways of trying to achieve these things were not skillful.

Encouraging Mr. Youngquist to express himself in words, because his use of language was improving, rather than inappropriate actions seemed a good idea to Maureen because she did not see his behavior as threatening or abusive. It appeared that he really did like her. Aside from the problem behavior, he usually was cooperative, friendly, and considerate.

Because active listening includes attending to nonverbal communication and restating or rephrasing what you think the person is saying, Maureen decided it might be helpful to use active listening in response to Mr. Youngquist's attempts to touch her. This might encourage the positive behavior of Mr. Youngquist's trying to use words to express himself rather than unwelcome actions. It would also be a change in the Consequence to the behavior, because the consequence that had been following the behavior (i.e., Maureen's telling Mr. Youngquist to stop) did not seem to help. In fact, because the challenging behavior continued after that consequence, the consequence most likely reinforced the behavior in some way. Maureen wondered if perhaps the consequence was a reinforcer because it was delivered in a way that suggested her underlying respect for, appreciation of, and interest in Mr. Youngquist.

Maureen decided to avoid his hand or gently redirect it while restating what his behavior seemed to mean and which feelings he seemed to have. Maureen thought she would say, "It is important to you to feel appreciated and valued, and you want me to feel that way, too," "You need me to know you like me. And it's important to you to know I like you," or, "You want to show me I'm important to you and you want to feel important to me." Maureen thought it might help to clearly state her preference for the expression of his warm feelings in other ways, perhaps by saying, "I'm flattered by your feelings for me, but it's not polite for you to touch me that way. Not touching me that way and being your usual friendly, cooperative, considerate self would be a nice way to show me you like me. You could also try to use words and tell me what I do that you like. And I guess I could also tell you a bit more about what you do that I like."

Results   Someone else assisted Maureen with Mr. Youngquist, as planned. Maureen and other staff members increasingly used social reinforcers to encourage his positive behaviors. As a result, Mr. Youngquist did not try to touch Maureen inappropriately again. Then, after several weeks of following the plan, unexpected staffing problems meant that Maureen ended up alone while helping Mr. Youngquist. She continued the positive comments and praise for his efforts in changing and getting to bed. When he expressed frustration at his ability, she used active listening. Mr. Youngquist did not touch her inappropriately. When Maureen spoke to Barbara about this development, they decided that Maureen could "go solo" with Mr. Youngquist again the next evening. That second evening was successful also. Maureen used social reinforcers and active listening, and Mr. Youngquist did not engage in the problem behavior. The third evening was the same. Maureen and Barbara decided that they would continue with Maureen's solo work with Mr. Youngquist. If the problem behavior came back, they could always repeat the successful steps that they had used before:

1. Use the ABCs of Behavior to carefully observe the behavior, its triggers, and its reinforcers.

2. Change the possible triggers or reinforcers, or change both.

3. Encourage positive behaviors by frequently using praise, compliments, active listening, and other social reinforcers.

Try completing Exercise 3.4 to emphasize how the ABCs of Behavior are important for uncovering triggers and reinforcers.

   Mr. Fenety   Mr. Fenety was 44 years old. Before being admitted to the nursing home, he had experienced long-term addiction to heroin. He used other drugs, too—he tried anything that he thought would get him high. Mr. Fenety had received medical treatment for several overdoses. The last time, he was found unresponsive and without a heartbeat. Paramedics got his heart started again; however, he had brain damage. The damage affected his sense of balance severely, so he needed a wheelchair. It also made his movements imprecise and jerky, which made it impossible for him to eat or dress on his own.

   Mr. Fenety often pressed the call button to ask when he was going to get his medication, even though his memory was apparently not affected by his brain damage. Frequently, he sat in the doorway of his room calling, "Nurse . . . nurse . . . nurse." However, when someone attended to him, he would say that he did not feel well but would not describe any specific pain or discomfort.

   In general, staff described Mr. Fenety as always complaining, demanding, and insulting. Mr. Fenety often screamed at staff, saying things such as, "Nobody around here does what they're supposed to do! I always have to tell everybody that I need things—they should know! You people don't know your jobs! You idiots are supposed to take care of me! I'll get your a—es fired!" According to information in his chart, Mr. Fenety had always behaved this way. Most staff members believed nothing would ever change that.

   Kay, a registered nurse (RN) who was a charge nurse, noticed that whenever certain staff members responded to Mr. Fenety's calls for assistance, he whined

Exercise 3.4

Photocopy the ABCs of Behavior Observation Form in the appendix. During the next week, use copies of the form to track one nursing home resident's problem behavior that happens frequently (at least daily). If you cannot do this by observing a resident, do it by observing someone else. At the end of the week, determine which changes you would recommend in the antecedents or consequences (or both) of the behavior in order to help reduce or eliminate the problem behavior. Record your recommendations in the space below.

about how nobody cared about him but did not scream at them. When other staff members, including Kay, told Mr. Fenety he would have to wait, he was likely to scream demands, insults, or threats.

Kay explained to Mr. Fenety that his frequent calling and his screaming were disruptive and inappropriate. She told him that he would have to be more patient. If he called, someone would come to him as soon as possible, but if he was calling for something that was not critically important, he might have to wait until other priorities were met. Mr. Fenety replied, "Get the hell outta here, b——." Kay shook her head and left.

Kay told staff she was concerned that responding to Mr. Fenety quickly when he called for no reason only rewarded his demand for attention. She explained that they would address Mr. Fenety's problem behavior by not giving him what he wanted when he wanted it when this was not immediately necessary for his care. The plan was to check on Mr. Fenety when he called, but if he did not need anything critical, he was to be told that he would be taken care of during routine care time. If he said anything insulting or screamed, he was to be told that his behavior was inappropriate. Staff members were then to tell him that they would come back when his behavior improved.

Staff followed this plan for approximately a month. Unfortunately, Mr. Fenety's difficult behavior worsened. Several times per day he had episodes of screaming insults, demands, and threats.

Kay talked with a charge nurse from another unit about the problem and was told about the ABCs of Behavior. It was hard for her to believe that anything would help, especially because of Mr. Fenety's history of addiction and his apparently long-standing behavior problems. Kay also thought that the existing behavior modification plan was appropriate; if it did not work, nothing but medication could. However, the consulting psychiatrist was reluctant to use medication in this case. Feeling at her wits' end, Kay decided to try to use the ABCs of Behavior approach.

Determining Antecedents and Consequences   Kay thought about what usually happened just before one of Mr. Fenety's episodes. Typically, the antecedent ("A") seemed to be that he would not receive attention quickly or would be told to wait. The resulting behavior ("B") was that he screamed demands, insults, or threats. The usual consequence ("C") was that staff members told him his behavior was inappropriate and that they would not deal with him until he stopped behaving abusively; then, they would leave him. Sometimes, though, staff had to provide the care necessary for Mr. Fenety's health and safety, such as changing a soiled undergarment or assisting when he fell down. In the end, then, Mr. Fenety got what staff thought he wanted—attention—even though it was only brief, negative, or necessary attention. It also seemed to Kay that the more negative attention Mr. Fenety received and the longer he was left to himself, the louder and more abusive his language became. So, the consequences of negative attention, being left alone, and getting attention when it was absolutely necessary seemed to be reinforcing Mr. Fenety's problem behavior. Maureen then recorded the possible ABCs of Behavior for Mr. Fenety's verbal abuse:

A Antecedent	B Behavior	C Consequence
Mr. Fenety's call was not responded to as quickly as he wanted or he was told he would have to wait.	Mr. Fenety screamed demands, insults, or threats.	Mr. Fenety received negative attention, was left alone, or received brief attention when needed for health or safety.

Changing Antecedents and Consequences   Kay recognized that by trying not to reward Mr. Fenety's difficult behavior, the staff was focusing on only the consequence ("C") part of the ABCs of Behavior. It seemed that perhaps getting any attention—even negative attention—was reinforcing Mr. Fenety's unpleasant behavior. Giving periodic attention following his difficult behavior was sometimes unavoidable, however, as care sometimes had to be provided to ensure that Mr. Fenety's health and safety were not at risk. Even if he was screaming, necessary care would have to be provided.

Kay decided to experiment with changing the antecedent ("A") and consequence ("C")—that is, to change the parts of the "A" and "C" that could be changed. She told the staff that she would try a new approach: That day, whenever Mr. Fenety called, she would try to get to him before he raised his voice. As she put this plan into action, Kay usually was able to get to Mr. Fenety before he engaged in problem behavior. At these times, Mr. Fenety generally asked about things such as when his medication or lunch would be coming, complained of some vague pain or discomfort, talked about what he did not like about other people, or talked about how no one seemed to care about him. Kay answered his questions and spent a minute or two using active listening. By responding to him in these ways, Kay was changing the "A" to Mr. Fenety's verbal abuse, and when she responded in these ways, he did not scream demands, insults, or threats.

Whenever Kay was not able to get to Mr. Fenety before he started raising his voice, she ignored the problem behavior and went to him anyway. Again, she usually spent a minute or two answering his questions and using active listening. By doing these things, Kay changed the "C" to his difficult behavior, and the episodes of the behavior were short and did not escalate.

During that day and the next one, Mr. Fenety raised his voice with Kay only two times per day. Previously, this behavior had been happening five or more times each day. When Mr. Fenety did raise his voice during Kay's experiment, it never reached the level of screaming. Mr. Fenety only threatened to get Kay fired once during the two days of Kay's experiment. Before she started the experiment, Mr. Fenety had been threatening Kay that way at least five times every day.

It is good that Kay did not just give up after the times Mr. Fenety did raise his voice or threaten her. However, she did start to think, "What's the use? He's never going to change. Nothing works." Still, she stuck with her plan when she noticed that the problem behaviors happened much less frequently than they had before she started her experiment. This is because correcting antecedents and consequences leads to a notable change in a challenging behavior.

Although Mr. Fenety's difficult behavior did not completely disappear, the improvement was encouraging. Kay spoke with the rest of the staff about the helpful changes to their original plan. Now, Kay asked everyone to do what she had done during her experiment: When Mr. Fenety called, someone was to go to him before he raised his voice too much. Even if he started raising his voice, he was to be attended to anyway, and the tone of his voice was to be ignored. His questions were to be answered, and his criticisms or complaints were to be met with active listening.

After 2 weeks of following the revised plan, Mr. Fenety never raised his voice with Kay. Other staff members reported that he rarely raised his voice with them, either. Apparently, he shouted seven times during the 2-week period. This was a major improvement because he had been screaming no less than five times a day before the change in the plan. In addition, the seven times that he did shout during the 2 weeks were the only times he threatened to get anyone fired. Kay and the rest of the staff had effectively helped Mr. Fenety with his problem behavior of screaming demands, insults, or threats.

Such dramatic change does not happen in all cases, usually because the antecedents or consequences are not managed as well as they need to be for improvement. Also, in many cases, problem behaviors return periodically. In other cases, continued improvement is desirable. In any of these instances, using the ABCs of Behavior again is usually helpful; those involved might more carefully look for correct "A"s and "C"s and then change the "A"s, the "C"s, or both the "A"s and the "C"s. This concept is illustrated by the continuing case involving Mr. Fenety.

Kay was encouraged by the way things improved with Mr. Fenety, but she recognized that he still called for assistance more than any resident in his unit. The things he called about were not immediate threats to his or anyone else's well-being. They were typically things that he was able to do for himself or questions to which he likely knew the answers. Sometimes this problem behavior of frequently calling for assistance made it hard to respond to Mr. Fenety because Kay and other staff were busy with other residents. Other times, the behavior made it hard for staff to respond quickly to other residents' needs. In addition, the behavior made it nearly impossible for a staff member to take a much-needed break. To address these issues, Kay had a conversation with Mr. Fenety.

"Please call for help only when you really need it," Kay began.

Mr. Fenety responded, "I don't see why I have to wait. I'm always the last one taken care of."

Kay said, "Mr. Fenety, you are not always the last one. What are we supposed to do—leave other patients who need us just to come and tell you what you already know, such as when your medication is coming?"

Mr. Fenety yelled, "I don't care about anyone else! I'm number one! Not you! Not anyone else!"

Kay saw that her direct confrontation of the problem was triggering Mr. Fenety's agitation, so she used active listening and said, "I guess you need to feel like you matter, like someone cares enough to treat you like you're number one." As she continued using active listening, Mr. Fenety quickly calmed down.

Trying to get Mr. Fenety to actively help correct something that he did not consider a problem did not seem likely to work. So Kay wondered if using the ABCs of Behavior could help. The first step was to use the ABCs to look at Mr. Fenety's problem behavior of frequently trying to get someone to attend to him.

A Antecedent	B Behavior	C Consequence
Mr. Fenety was alone in his room.	Mr. Fenety started pushing the call button or calling, "Nurse . . . nurse . . . nurse."	A staff member went to Mr. Fenety.

Earlier experience with Mr. Fenety showed Kay that changing "C" could lead to increased problems. She and others on staff saw that not going to Mr. Fenety triggered greater difficulty—that is, his screaming demands, threats, or insults. Going to Mr. Fenety triggered less problematic behavior; rather than persistently screaming, he simply continued to call out or use the call button often. Although this was an improvement, going to Mr. Fenety after he called out or used the call button did reinforce that particular behavior.

Changing the Antecedent   Kay decided that it might be a good idea to try changing the antecedent to Mr. Fenety's problem behavior of frequently trying to get someone to attend to him. Because being alone in his room usually came before his calling for assistance, Kay guessed that being alone in his room was a trigger. Mr. Fenety rarely used the call bell or called out while someone (e.g., visitors, other residents, staff) was with him, and he did it most often in the evening until about 9:00 P.M., at which time he usually settled down for the night.

Kay was working evenings, so she decided to try another experiment. Each evening, the first thing she did was go into Mr. Fenety's room. She was usually able to do this before he called out or used the call bell. For a week, she also went to see Mr. Fenety every 20 minutes from after dinner until 9:00 P.M. It was difficult to do this because Kay had other responsibilities; however, a couple of other staff members helped out enough that Kay had time to try her plan.

When she went into Mr. Fenety's room, Kay usually just asked how he was or engaged in small talk with him. Mr. Fenety still had a tendency to complain, so Kay used active listening with him often. Kay usually limited these visits to no more than 2 minutes. Sometimes Mr. Fenety asked Kay for help with activities that he was able to do independently. Kay noticed that when she helped, Mr. Fenety still did most other things he could do for himself.

Kay's brief visits to Mr. Fenety's room seemed to work very well. During the first week of following this plan, Mr. Fenety called out or used the call bell much less frequently during the evenings. Previously, he engaged in this behavior eight or more times every evening; after Kay began her visits, Mr. Fenety never called more than twice in an evening. In fact, Mr. Fenety did not call out or use the call bell even once during the last two evenings of the week.

After Kay began following her plan, she did feel disappointed whenever Mr. Fenety called for assistance. However, she remembered that his behavior really had improved. This is an important point. Behavior change is often gradual. Also, problem behavior occasionally increases when a resident feels stressed by a worsening physical condition, a move to a new room, a roommate dying, or other changes in routines or important relationships (e.g., changes in staff due to turnover or scheduling). Thus, although behavior change is often not fast and complete, it is important to recognize improvements. Acknowledge your partial successes and those of the resident. They are steps along the way to the best possible outcome. Display 3.4 lists realistic and unrealistic goals regarding the improvement of challenging behaviors.

Continuing Success   Kay spoke with the rest of the staff about her findings. By the next week, it became routine for more staff to briefly but frequently shoot the breeze with Mr. Fenety. Staff members were typically able to stop by before he called out. Active listening was usually all he needed when he complained about his health or other people. When he asked for help, it was usually for something that could be addressed and did not interfere with his ability to do things independently. At the end of the second week, Mr. Fenety's behavior continued to improve. Most evenings he did not call out at all. When he did engage in this behavior, he only did so once or twice per evening.

As the other staff members helped out in this way, Kay gradually cut back how often she visited Mr. Fenety. On the first night of the second week, she went to his room every 25 minutes. The next night she visited every 30 minutes. Kay decided that visiting Mr. Fenety every 30 minutes would not interfere with her other work or burden her.

Kay also realized that in the future, other staff members could gradually increase the amount of time between their visits to Mr. Fenety. They could do this until they found the most workable balance between Mr. Fenety's need for social interaction and their need to do other things.

Visiting Mr. Fenety before he called for assistance reinforced his behavior of quietly watching television, which is what he was usually doing when staff came to visit. The "B" in the ABCs of Mr. Fenety's evening behavior became "sitting quietly." The "C" (reinforcing consequence) became the social interaction of having staff visit, use active listening, chat, or respond to what was usually a small request for help. In this case, the "A" (triggering antecedent) to Mr. Fenety's quiet behavior was his not being alone in his room for longer than he was able to tolerate. By gradually *stretching* the time between their visits to Mr. Fenety, staff members were also helping him to stretch his ability to tolerate being alone to a more mutually agreeable point. The technique of stretching can be useful in working with nursing home residents who are demanding or frequently seek attention (see Display 3.5).

Realistic Goals for Residents' Problem Behaviors

We are likely to have unrealistic goals when we

- Expect problem behaviors to never happen

- Expect a problem behavior that happens frequently to go away immediately

- Expect a very intense problem behavior to completely stop right away

- Consider problem behaviors as simply wrong and as things that are not supposed to happen

We can develop realistic goals for helping residents change difficult behaviors when we

- Remember that problem behaviors sometimes change gradually

- Remember to look for decreased frequency of problem behaviors

- Remember to look for decreased intensity of problem behaviors when they do occur

- Remember to look for shorter episodes of problem behaviors

Having unrealistic goals can lead us to

- Believe that nothing works and that nothing will change

- Give up on effective ways of dealing with challenging behavior

- Feel helpless, angry, and burned out

Having realistic goals can

- Help us stay focused on effective ways of dealing with problem behaviors

Caring for People with Challenging Behaviors: Essential Skills and Successful Strategies in Long-Term Care
© 2005 Stephen Weber Long. Published by Health Professions Press, Inc. (http://www.healthpropress.com).
All rights reserved.

Stretching

Stretching is a way of helping residents improve demanding or disruptive attention-seeking behavior. It helps by gradually lengthening the amount of time they can go without responses to concerns that are not immediately critical for anyone's health or well-being.

Step 1

A. Make it routine to go to the resident *before* he or she calls out, shouts, or makes demands. Initially, this can mean going to the resident quite often.

B. Go to the resident regardless of whether you can reach him or her before demanding or attention-seeking behavior occurs.

C. If the resident makes demands, respond as though the demand is a reasonable, polite request. Do what you can to respond to the resident's request, assuming that doing so does not pose an immediate risk to the health or well-being of the resident or anyone else.

D. If the resident complains, argues, hurls insults, or makes verbal threats, use listening skills. In addition, use social reinforcers such as praise, compliments, thumbs-up signs, pats on the back, or hugs for *any* positive behavior.

Step 2

A. Once you establish a pattern of getting to the resident *before* demanding or disruptive attention-seeking behavior starts, you will probably see a decrease in the behavior within a few days. If there is no significant decrease after 2 weeks, it is likely that the person has not consistently been attended to *before* the problem behavior starts.

B. Once a pattern has been established and there has been a significant decrease in the problem behavior, stay with the plan for 3–7 days. Then, begin gradually stretching the amount of time between your visits by a few minutes — probably by no more than 5 minutes at the beginning.

C. If the problem behavior does not significantly increase after a day of stretching, the next day try stretching the time between visits by a few more minutes. Each day, gradually stretch the amount of time until you determine what length of time the resident is currently able to tolerate.

(continued)

D.   If the problem behavior increases in frequency or severity, begin again with Step 1. This time, lengthen the amount of time between visits more gradually. Make the increases in the length of time between visits smaller. Wait 2 or more days before making further increases.

E.   If you try the stretching process twice and it does not help, try it again and watch carefully for triggers and reinforcers of the problem behavior. Record your observations of what is happening to or around the resident before and after the behavior starts.

Caring for People with Challenging Behaviors: Essential Skills and Successful Strategies in Long-Term Care

COOPERATIVE PROBLEM SOLVING WITH RESIDENTS

The ABCs of Behavior approach is particularly helpful when a resident does not realize or acknowledge that there is a problem or when a resident cannot change elements of the situations that trigger or reinforce the problem behavior. Another approach to challenging behavior actively involves a resident in finding solutions. This problem-solving approach starts with the use of active listening. We restate what we hear the resident saying and name the feelings the resident seems to be having, to the degree that the resident is able to tolerate. We say in our own words what the resident seems to be naming as the problem.

Next, we ask the resident if there are times when the problematic situation does not occur, and if so, what the surrounding circumstances are. Considering this information can give the resident a chance to think about and describe what can be done to adjust the problem situation. We wonder together which actions taken by the resident and by others contribute to situations in which the problem is prevented or eliminated. If necessary or helpful, we can also encourage the resident to reminisce about similar problems in his or her past. We can ask questions such as, "Have you always felt this frightened?" or "Have you never felt safe?" By including the words *always* and *never,* we may trigger a person's memories of how similar problems happened in the past, how they do not always happen, and how the resident previously coped with them.

Ms. Quigley

We met 77-year-old Ms. Quigley in Chapter 1. She had severe difficulty breathing, was very anxious, and often called for someone to come to her room. She called so frequently that it was difficult for staff to attend to her and accomplish their other responsibilities.

Peggy, a social worker, visited Ms. Quigley to see what could be done about these frequent calls for attention. When Ms. Quigley asked Peggy to take the cover off the lunch tray that was right in front of her—something Ms. Quigley was able to do herself—Peggy did it. When Ms. Quigley complained of how no one understood how sick she was and how much help she needed, Peggy used active listening. When Ms. Quigley spoke about her fear of being alone and her constant anxiety, Peggy continued using active listening.

Ms. Quigley still seemed nervous, her hands quickly moving among the plates and utensils on her tray without any apparent purpose other than to touch them or move them slightly one way and then another. However, she was noticeably less nervous than when Peggy had first walked into the room.

Peggy asked, "I know you were just saying that you always feel anxious, Ms. Quigley, but are there times when you don't feel as anxious as you can get?"

Ms. Quigley explained, "I feel less anxious now that you're here listening to me."

Peggy then asked, "Have you always had a problem with anxiety?"

Ms. Quigley responded, "I was high-strung from an early age. I used to deal with it by being active. I was always very social when I was young, going to parties and dances, spending time with my friends and on the telephone, and being involved in church activities."

"What has helped you since you haven't been able to be as active as you used to be?" Peggy asked.

Ms. Quigley said, "When I'm around other people, even if I'm just watching them as they walk past or do other things, I'm less anxious. Talking to someone who will really just listen is the most help."

Peggy and Ms. Quigley then spoke with the charge nurse. They arranged to have an oxygen tank put on Ms. Quigley's wheelchair and to let her spend time each day near the front door in the lobby, where she would see staff, visitors, and other residents coming and going. The plan included assistance in getting Ms. Quigley to the lobby. It also included two 15-minute visits per week from Peggy so Ms. Quigley could talk to someone who would "really just listen."

Mr. Dukmejian

Late one night, 72-year-old Mr. Dukmejian threw a trash basket. It smashed against a wall in the hallway. This occurred after a couple of weeks of his being increasingly active and noisy in his room at night, playing his radio loudly and singing. Ray, the new night charge nurse, went to talk with Mr. Dukmejian.

Mr. Dukmejian talked about needing to keep "those strange people" out of his room at night. Ray used active listening, rephrasing and restating what Mr. Dukmejian said, and commented that Mr. Dukmejian seemed frightened. Mr. Dukmejian continued by saying it really was not safe for him to go to sleep with people coming in to "go to the bathroom" on the floor in his room. He was afraid they would beat him up and have sex with him, he said. "And I'm not even gay," Mr. Dukmejian asserted.

"Are there times when they don't come into your room at night?" Ray asked.

Mr. Dukmejian pointed out, "They're not around now, while we're talking."

Ray asked, "Has nighttime always been frightening for you?"

Mr. Dukmejian explained, "When I was growing up, I shared a room with my older brothers. Then, after I got married, my wife and I shared the same bed for 50 years. So, no, I never was scared at night."

Ray commented, "Knowing there are people around that you feel safe with seems to help. What can you do when you wake up at night and do not feel safe?"

Mr. Dukmejian said he was not sure, so Ray suggested, "You seem to feel safe with me as we talk. If you wake up at night and feel frightened or if those people come back, maybe you could come sit near the nurses' station while I work."

Mr. Dukmejian replied, "That's a good idea."

Mr. Dukmejian and Ray worked together to resolve the problematic situation. See Display 3.6 for a summary of this approach. Try completing Exercise 3.5 to learn more about personal applications of this method.

Cooperative Problem Solving

It is often helpful to encourage a resident's active involvement in resolving problems that trigger or reinforce problem behaviors. Using the following five steps can foster cooperative problem solving with residents:

1. Use the active listening techniques of rephrasing or restating what the resident seems to be saying verbally and nonverbally. Name the resident's feelings to the degree that the resident can tolerate. Using these techniques can help us understand the problem from the resident's perspective.

2. Ask the resident if there are times when what he or she considers the problem does not happen. What are the circumstances when the problem does not exist? What do others do that prevents or stops the problem? What does the resident do that prevents or stops the problem?

3. If needed or helpful, encourage the resident to think back in his or her life. Ask things such as, "Have you always felt _____?," "Has it never been any different at any time in your life?," or "What helped when things such as this happened (or when you felt this way) in the past?"

4. Use the resident's replies in Steps 2 and 3 to decide with him or her what to do in the current situation.

5. Sometimes the cooperative problem-solving method does not work. If the resident does not or is not able to cooperate or if his or her behavior worsens during the cooperative problem-solving process, try to determine what might be triggering or reinforcing the behavior.

Caring for People with Challenging Behaviors: Essential Skills and Successful Strategies in Long-Term Care

Exercise 3.5

Think of an incident in which a nursing home resident engaged in a difficult behavior. If you cannot think of an incident involving a resident, think of one involving someone else.

Briefly describe the behavior.

Briefly describe the following:

1. How you used or could have used active listening and what the other person seemed to consider as the problem

2. How you asked or could have asked the person about times when the problematic situation does not happen

3. How you encouraged or could have encouraged the person to think of past experiences when the problem — as that person saw it — did not exist or when the problem was dealt with effectively

4. How you used or could have used the person's replies in Steps 2 and 3 to help reduce or eliminate his or her difficult behavior

5. What you did or might have done if cooperative problem-solving steps were not helpful with this person

COPING WITH STRESS BY USING MENTAL IMAGERY

As noted, how we cope with stress can have a significant impact on how we react to difficult behavior. Chapter 2 explained how practicing relaxation techniques for 10–20 minutes each day can help reduce our overall level of stress. That chapter also described the relaxation method of progressive muscle relaxation. This chapter explores the technique of mental imagery.

Mental imagery can be used by itself or in combination with other relaxation techniques, such as progressive muscle relaxation. To use mental imagery, sit or lie comfortably in a spot where you will not be disturbed for 10–20 minutes. Imagine yourself in a pleasant, relaxing place. See, hear, feel, and smell the things that make it a peaceful place. See the colors and shapes of things and the gentle movements. Hear the sounds. Feel the comforting touch of a soft breeze, the "just right" temperature, or the sensation of your body being supported or perhaps even floating. Smell the fragrances. (See Display 3.7 for a step-by-step description of the mental imagery process.)

For example, see yourself at the beach on a day when the temperature is comfortably warm. The sky is beautifully clear and blue, with occasional puffy white clouds that drift slowly over the ocean. There are a few people here and there, strolling or lying on the sand. A gentle, warm breeze brushes your face as you walk barefoot on the sand. You feel the sand massage your feet with each step that you take. The breeze has a clean, fresh, mildly salty fragrance. You stop walking, stretch out on the sand, and look up at a few clouds against the blue sky. The warm sand supports your body as it conforms to the contours of your back and your legs. Watching the clouds drift lazily by, you hear the distant, occasional sounds of children happily playing and a seagull's cry. As the sights, sounds, and scents of this place deepen your relaxation, feel the weight of your body against the sand get pleasantly heavier as you become more deeply relaxed.

Continue your relaxation session for the time you have set aside. When the time is up, gently stretch your arms, legs, and neck before going on with your day.

SUMMARY

Chapter 3 discussed how behaviors, whether positive or negative, happen for reasons. It also described ways of finding solutions to residents' difficult behaviors. The first is the ABCs of Behavior method. The ABCs of Behavior concept has the following elements:

A: Every behavior has at least one *antecedent,* or thing that precedes it and serves as a trigger.

B: A *behavior* is any action.

C: If a behavior continues or gets stronger, at least one *consequence,* or thing that comes after the behavior, is a reinforcer.

Mental Imagery

You can use this relaxation technique alone or in conjunction with other relaxation techniques. Remember, practicing relaxation techniques for 10–20 minutes per day can be very helpful in managing the negative effects of stress on your mental and physical health.

1. Sit or lie in a comfortable position where you will not be disturbed for 10–20 minutes. Close your eyes and imagine yourself in a pleasant, relaxing place, such as a beach, a park, or a forest with a stream — any place that you find relaxing.

2. In your mind, see the things that make the place you have chosen a comforting place. You might see the pleasant way the sunlight sparkles on water, the soft green of a patch of grass, or curtains stirred by a slight breeze.

3. Hear the relaxing sounds of the place you have in mind. They might be a light breeze rustling the uppermost leaves of the trees, birds singing, or the sounds of a meal being prepared in the kitchen.

4. Feel what is comforting about the place. You might feel the warmth of the sun, the weight of your body as you are stretched out in the grass, or the coziness of wearing a sweater.

5. Notice the fragrances. These might be the scent of fresh earth, flowers, or a favorite meal being made.

Become aware of the sights, sounds, and sensations that you find comforting about your peaceful, relaxing place. As you do, enjoy the experience of becoming more pleasantly at ease, calm, and relaxed.

By carefully observing what happens before and after a behavior, we can determine the likely triggering antecedents and reinforcing consequences that need to be changed in order for the behavior to change.

The second method of finding solutions to difficult behaviors is cooperative problem solving. The steps of the cooperative problem-solving method described are as follows:

1. Use active listening to get a clear idea of what the resident sees as the problematic situation.

2. Ask the resident about what is happening when the problem is not present, if there are such times.

3. Ask the resident to reminisce about times in his or her life when the problem was prevented or coped with and how.

4. Use the resident's replies in Steps 2 and 3 to decide with him or her how to deal with current difficulties.

5. If the cooperative problem-solving method does not work, use the ABCs of Behavior approach.

Chapter 3 also described the technique of stretching. This technique is based on the ABCs of Behavior. It can be very helpful for dealing with a resident who is demanding or frequently engages in disruptive attention-seeking behavior. Stretching involves two steps. First, routinely go to the resident *before* the problem behavior occurs, ignore the behavior if it happens, respond to the resident's request, and use praise and other social reinforcers for any behavior that is not a problem behavior. Second, gradually increase the amount of time between routine visits to the resident to stretch his or her ability to tolerate not being the focus of attention for longer periods of time.

In addition, this chapter discussed setting realistic goals. We work toward realistic goals for helping a resident reduce or eliminate a problem behavior when we help decrease the frequency of the behavior, the intensity of the behavior, or both. For some residents, a reasonable goal may simply be that when episodes occur, they are briefer in duration. Remember that improvement is often gradual. It is best to work on reducing or eliminating only one or two problem behaviors at a time.

This chapter also encouraged us to contain our own strong emotional reactions that are possible when we face residents' challenging behavior. Such emotions often reflect the feelings that overwhelm residents. By containing these feelings and behaving in the nonaggressive, helpful ways that we would like to see from residents, we shoulder some of the burden of their feelings and perhaps encourage them to improve their behavior.

Finally, Chapter 3 further explored the concept of addressing stress among nursing home staff. The stress management technique of mental imagery was detailed.

Chapter 4

Stress and the Roles of Thinking and Feeling

One of the most important ways of effectively dealing with residents' behavior problems is coping with how we feel about what they do. The strength of what we feel affects how we react when a resident behaves in demanding, insulting, threatening, agitated, confused, or depressed ways. Some of our feelings while addressing problem behavior include frustration, anger, hopelessness, depression, confusion, and even fear. Our stress is often due to one or more of these feelings. These emotions are very real and can have a significant impact on our mental and physical health.

This book's techniques for helping reduce or eliminate problem behaviors can help us manage stress. Often, believing that we know what to do can make a difficult situation less stressful. The techniques in *Caring for People with Challenging Behaviors* can also help because they can effectively reduce or eliminate the situations that we find stressful. The stress management techniques can help, too.

As nursing home staff members, we can expect to face problem behaviors. With some residents, reducing—not eliminating—a problem behavior may be the only realistic short-term goal. The longer-term goal might be to further reduce the problem. Staff members need to cope with their reactions to the difficult behavior on the way to that goal. How we manage our reactions to the problem behavior can have a major impact on how reachable that goal is.

This chapter looks at the link between thinking and feeling and how it can be used to help us deal with the stress of working in a nursing home. In addition, the chapter further explores how our own feelings can be clues for best responding to difficult behavior. Chapter 4 ends by describing another relaxation method to use during a quiet time in your day. This simple method focuses on breathing to deepen relaxation as a stress management technique.

THINKING AND FEELING EXPLAINED

Thinking and feeling are connected: How we feel affects how we think, and how we think affects how we feel. If we feel too frightened, anxious, angry, or excited, our thinking can become confused. If we frequently think things such as, "I'm not good at anything. Nobody ever really cares about me," we are likely to feel hopeless and depressed.

To deal effectively with stressful situations such as working with residents who behave in difficult ways, it is important for us to try to recognize and manage our own feelings and thoughts about what residents do. This can be a challenge because it is not always easy to be aware of our emotions. Many of us, for example, have been taught that we should not feel angry. Some of us have taken that lesson so much to heart that even when our heads are pounding and our hearts are racing, even when we are sweating and we are shouting, we insist, "I AM NOT ANGRY!"

It is also difficult to be aware of some of the things we believe. Often, we take what we believe so much for granted that the way we look at things just seems to be the way that things must be. Our thoughts can be so automatic that we cannot imagine seeing things any other way. For example, we may have the unnoticed automatic belief that a nice person does not get angry, that we must always be nice people, and so we must never be angry. Such a set of beliefs leaves us at risk of not being able to acknowledge reasonable and natural reasons for feeling angry. Such a set of beliefs also leaves us at risk of not allowing ourselves to recognize signals from our bodies or behavior that we are angry. Not recognizing the signals and not acknowledging the feelings can lead to not knowing how our behavior is motivated by what we feel. However, knowing what we feel and why can help us more effectively deal with problems that contribute to stress.

Becoming Aware of Emotions

A helpful step to becoming aware of stressful emotions is paying attention to how our bodies feel. Common signs of emotions that might be difficult to acknowledge include a pounding or racing heart, shallow or rapid breathing, headaches, sweating, tension in the neck and shoulders, clenched teeth, and stomachaches. Of course, if you are troubled by these symptoms and are concerned that they may be signs of illness—or if they cause you significant pain or interfere with your work, social or family life, or recreation—consult a health care professional. Even if these symptoms are related to an illness and you do get appropriate professional attention, it is helpful to examine how they may also be affected by unacknowledged emotions.

Some of our behaviors also signal that we are trying to deal with emotions of which we are unaware. For example, if we are raising our voices, scolding, sarcastically teasing others, ignoring or avoiding a person, withholding things from someone, or acting impatient, we may very well be angry.

Recognizing signals such as these tells us that it may be good to take steps to deal differently with the things that are having such a negative impact.

THE ABCs OF THINKING AND FEELING

The ABCs of Thinking and Feeling is a method of using what we know about emotions and thoughts to help us cope with the stress we can feel when facing residents' challenging behavior. It assists us in looking at how our thinking can add to our stress and can help us reduce our stress. The basic idea in the ABCs of Thinking and Feeling is that when we think differently about something, we feel differently. For example, if you thought the person next to you in a crowd intentionally pushed you, you would be likely to feel differently than if you believed the person accidentally stumbled.

In the ABCs of Thinking and Feeling, "A" stands for **A**ctivating Event. This phrase reminds us that our thoughts and feelings are related to some action that happens to us or around us or that we find out about—some activating event. The previous example of a person pushing you is an example of an activating event.

The "B" stands for **B**eliefs, or our thoughts about the action. In the previous example, your beliefs might have been, "It was rude, mean, and obnoxious for that person to push me! That person should not do that! That person has no right to do that! It is just plain wrong!"

The "C" stands for the emotional **C**onsequences of our beliefs. Anger can be the emotional consequence of thinking that a person intentionally pushed you. Other emotional consequences include feeling stressed or upset. Even if we do not use words such as *angry, stressed,* or *upset,* feeling flushed or having a pounding or racing heart, or breathing rapidly can be the emotional consequences of the action. See Display 4.1 for additional information.

Anger and the ABCs of Thinking and Feeling

Residents' challenging behaviors can result in feelings of anger among staff. This is particularly the case when the behaviors are directed specifically toward staff.

Belinda and Mr. Putin   Belinda had heard of the ABCs of Thinking and Feeling. When Mr. Putin yelled, "You're a G—d——— b——," however, what went through her mind was, "Beliefs?! Thoughts?! I don't have any thoughts—I am just furious!"

The ABCs of Thinking and Feeling

It is important to cope with how we feel about residents who behave in difficult ways and about the behaviors themselves. Often, what we feel can be described as stress. This usually means that we are having unpleasant emotions such as anger, frustration, hopelessness, depression, anxiety, and fear. Or, it might mean we have problems such as fatigue, muscle tension, headaches, an upset stomach, or a racing or pounding heart. (If any such symptoms are significant, speak to a health care professional.) Our thoughts influence our emotions — that is, they influence how we feel.

A Our thoughts and feelings are related to an **A**ctivating Event — something that happens to us or around us or that we find out about.

A nursing home resident, Mrs. Bidwell, pulled away from Janice, a nursing assistant, and tried to hit her.

B **B**eliefs are our thoughts about the activating event.

Janice might think, "That no-good b——! She's always trouble!" Or perhaps Janice could think, "I must not be doing what I should. I must be doing an awful job if I do it so bad that Mrs. Bidwell tries to hit me. I'm not good at anything."

C In turn, there are emotional **C**onsequences of what we think or believe about something that happened.

If Janice thinks of Mrs. Bidwell as "a no-good b——" and a troublemaker, anger is a possible emotional consequence of what she thinks. If Janice thinks that she is doing an awful job and is not good at anything, depression could be the emotional consequence of what she thinks.

Caring for People with Challenging Behaviors: Essential Skills and Successful Strategies in Long-Term Care

Later, at a calmer moment, she tried to use the ABCs of Thinking and Feeling to examine what happened. The "A" was easy for Belinda to identify: "Putin called me a G—d——— b——." The "C" was easy for her to identify, too: anger. Yet, it was not as easy for her to discern her thoughts about what Mr. Putin did. "It doesn't even make sense to ask what *my* beliefs are about what *he* did," she said to herself. "It is obvious he has no right to do that. He always treats me like filth. He never acts like a human being. No matter what I do for him, he is never satisfied. I get so furious just thinking about it!"

Then Belinda realized that what she had been saying to herself constituted her beliefs. She recognized that she felt increasingly angry when she thought about what Mr. Putin did. Her beliefs ("B") were so automatic, she had not even been considering them as thoughts. The fact that thinking about the incident increased her anger was a clue that Mr. Putin's action was not the only factor. How Belinda thought about the incident had a lot to do with how furious she felt.

A few days later Mr. Putin called Belinda the same name while she was helping him to bed. She was startled and a little angry, then the anger quickly passed and she felt fairly calm. She responded to Mr. Putin by saying, "You're pretty angry with me." Then she listened to him complain without trying to correct him. She knew that trying to reason with a very agitated person is not a good way of de-escalating the situation.

As Mr. Putin complained, Belinda said things such as, "Oh," and "I guess I'm not very helpful sometimes," and "Um-hmm," and "It sounds like nobody ever does what you want." Belinda noticed that although he continued complaining, Mr. Putin stopped shouting and cooperated as she finished helping him. In fact, he soon stopped complaining, and he said, "Thank you" when Belinda was done.

Looking at what happened in this case, the "A," or the activating event, was again Mr. Putin's calling Belinda a bad name. The "C," or emotional consequence, was that Belinda felt startled and a little angry but then felt fairly calm. The emotional consequences were the result of the "B," or the beliefs or thoughts, that went through Belinda's mind in reaction to Mr. Putin's strong language. A number of thoughts went through her mind in reaction to what Mr. Putin said:

- "Who does he think he's treating this way? He should not talk to me like that!" (This was her first reaction, after which she started to feel angry. Then she had other thoughts.)

- "Someone who acts this way has somehow learned to expect that he must be abusive to get what he wants or needs. His doing that is more likely to push people he needs away . . . or get them to retaliate."

- "He must expect that I will only pay attention if he is abusive."

- "He doesn't really know me. I make mistakes sometimes, but that doesn't make me a G—d——— b——."

- "He acts this way sometimes."

- "Yesterday we joked together while I helped him to bed. Maybe we will to-morrow, too."

Belinda's thoughts about Mr. Putin and his behavior eventually helped her avoid the stress of a very strong angry reaction. Her beliefs helped her to avoid feeling very angry and to remain fairly calm. This in turn helped her deal with the situation effectively.

Depression and the ABCs of Thinking and Feeling

Depression is a difficult emotional experience that also can easily be triggered by working with nursing home patients. It is characterized by such feelings as worthlessness, hopelessness, and guilt. Those suffering from depression might describe their mood as down or blue. Frequently, they have trouble sleeping and eating—either too much or too little in both cases. People with depression often have little or no pleasure in things they once found pleasurable. In severe cases, there can be a preoccupation with thoughts of death and suicide.

Louisa and Mrs. Floyd   Louisa was on her way to help a resident when she walked past Mrs. Floyd, who was sitting in a wheelchair in the doorway of her room. Mrs. Floyd asked if Louisa could help her to the dining room. Louisa said she would be back to do that in a few minutes. However, the other resident had a toileting mishap, so he and his clothing were quite soiled. After Louisa helped him get cleaned and changed, she rushed back toward the dining room to help residents who needed assistance eating, forgetting that she said she would help Mrs. Floyd to the dining room. While Louisa was helping another resident eat, she saw Mrs. Floyd wheel herself—slowly and with great effort—through the dining room door. Louisa then remembered her assurance of help and thought, "How horrible that I forgot. This is terrible, awful. I should not forget when I give my word that I will do something. I am undependable. I am unreliable." With these thoughts, she felt guilty and bad about herself.

In the past, Louisa had suffered from rather severe depression. When she was most depressed, an incident like forgetting to go back for Mrs. Floyd would have triggered increasingly intense depressive thoughts. At those times, her thoughts created a downward spiral, pulling her deeper into depression. At those times, she had thoughts resembling those about the incident with Mrs. Floyd, but they were followed by other thoughts such as, "I should be ashamed of myself. I'm not good at my job. I don't do what I'm supposed to do. What I did to Mrs. Floyd was unforgivable." Such thinking made Louisa feel more than guilty; she would begin to feel worthless and irredeemably sinful. However, she had since learned about the ABCs of Thinking and Feeling and decided to use this technique instead.

The first step, being aware of how she felt, came most easily for Louisa. It was also easy for her to know that forgetting to go back to Mrs. Floyd was the activating event that triggered her negative feelings. She had no trouble identifying the thoughts that followed the activating event, either. Louisa recorded her ABCs of Thinking and Feeling as follows.

A Activating event	B Beliefs	C Emotional consequences
I forgot to go back and help Mrs. Floyd get to the dining room.	How horrible that I forgot. This is terrible, awful. I should not forget when I give my word that I will do something. I am undepend-able. I am unreliable.	I felt guilty and bad about myself—a bit down.

ABC . . . D Louisa went on to an additional step in the ABCs of Thinking and Feeling: "D." That is, she **D**isputed the thoughts that were getting her down. To do this, she wondered whether her thoughts were based on facts or whether they were just coming out of persistent beliefs. Louisa decided to look at the evidence supporting her thoughts related to the "A," or the activating event, of her forgetting to go back to Mrs. Floyd. She also decided to consider other ways of thinking about what happened.

"Was it really horrible, terrible, or awful that I forgot? Was anyone badly hurt? Was anything significantly damaged?" Louisa wondered. No one was physically hurt and nothing was broken, she had to admit. Louisa recognized that she was "catastrophizing" the situation. It would be more realistic to say that she wished the incident with Mrs. Floyd had not happened rather than to consider it a catastrophe.

Louisa realized that Mrs. Floyd might have felt disappointed, angry, or down about being forgotten. She thought, "It is true that if Mrs. Floyd were forgotten like this often, it would be bad for her mental and physical health." Yet, Louisa could not recall ever having overlooked Mrs. Floyd before.

At this point in her thinking, Louisa thought, "Still, Mrs. Floyd must be very angry with me. I can't bear that. I really shouldn't do things that make anybody angry. I need people to like me." Louisa saw she was catastrophizing again, even though she was not thinking the words *terrible, horrible,* or *awful.* Louisa concluded that it was not the end of the world if Mrs. Floyd got angry with her; it might be unfortunate but understandable and survivable.

Louisa noticed that she was also "shoulding." She was insisting that she should never do things that upset others. "Do I really have to not upset anyone?" she asked herself. It seemed to her that she was holding herself to an unrealistic standard. It would be more reasonable to see that not everyone will always be happy with everything she does. She has human limitations to her abilities and can therefore be expected to disappoint others at times. This is not necessarily hor-rible, terrible, catastrophic, or a sign that she is worthless or bad.

Louisa then considered her thought, "I need people to like me." When she thought this, she was assuming that if someone, such as Mrs. Floyd, got angry with her, that meant the person did not like her. "If someone is angry with me for something I did, that doesn't necessarily mean that person will always be angry with me or dislike me forever," she realized. The more Louisa thought about it, the more she recognized that she was overgeneralizing. She was jumping from the idea that Mrs. Floyd would not like her to the fear that no one would. At this point Louisa thought, "Even if Mrs. Floyd doesn't like me, that doesn't mean that no one else will. It would be better if Mrs. Floyd liked me—I would really prefer that—but if she doesn't, there are other people who do."

Finally, Louisa examined the thought, "I am undependable. I am unreliable." She recognized that she was labeling herself as completely undependable and to-tally unreliable. It was true that forgetting to go back to Mrs. Floyd was not a de-pendable or reliable act. However, that did not mean that Louisa always forgot to do what she said she would. It did not mean she always would forget to do such things, either. Even if Louisa did behave in undependable or unreliable ways often, she could take steps to change that.

While thinking that she was undependable or unreliable, Louisa was ignoring all of the times that she followed through on her word. Louisa recognized that she had been using a "mental filter," filtering out of her awareness the times when she behaved in dependable and reliable ways. She was using selective attention, notic-ing only what was negative. When Louisa saw this, she made it a point to recall her positive behaviors, such as helping the resident who had the toileting acci-dent. She also did not forget to help out in the dining room. In fact, Louisa recalled many times during the day when she behaved dependably and reliably.

Disputing her initial depressing thoughts helped Louisa feel less guilty and bad about herself. She even felt less stressed; she did not feel as overwhelmed and tired. Display 4.2 provides a summary of the process in which Louisa engaged.

Common Unhelpful Habits of Thinking

Louisa's initial unhelpful thoughts fell into some common patterns. When we are most stressed and troubled by strong feelings such as depression, anger, or anxi-ety, we are likely to think in these or similar ways. We are likely to feel most stressed when we see ourselves, others, or situations in completely negative ways. When we do this, we are thinking in "either-or," "all-or-nothing" ways. Louisa did this when she labeled herself completely unreliable because she forgot to help Mrs. Floyd. At that time, Louisa believed she could only be either reliable or un-reliable. There was no being partly or usually reliable; it was all or nothing. Be-linda was thinking in a similar "either-or," "all-or-nothing" way when she labeled Mr. Putin as someone who never acts like a human being. At that time, Belinda believed that a person either behaved like a human being or not. There was no al-lowance for sometimes or mostly behaving like a human being; again, it was all or nothing.

The ABC . . . Ds of Thinking and Feeling

A   Our thoughts and feelings are related to **A**ctivating events — things that happen to us or around us or that we find out about.

B   Beliefs are our thoughts about the activating event.

C   In turn, there are emotional **C**onsequences of what we think or believe about something that happened.

D   We can stop and question — that is, re-evaluate and **D**ispute — the thoughts or beliefs that led to our stressful feelings.

The focus of this type of thinking affects whether we feel depressed or angry. When we focus the negative thoughts more on ourselves, we are likely to feel depressed. When our negative thoughts are focused on others, we are inclined to be angry. Any persistent or strong feelings that are harmful to our well-being, relationships, or work are likely to result from, or be contributed to by "either-or," "all-or-nothing" thinking. This includes feelings such as anxiety.

This does not mean that emotions such as depression, anger, and anxiety can or even should be completely eliminated. They are natural, expectable feelings. It makes sense to be angry about some things. It makes sense to be depressed or anxious about some things, too. Eliminating such feelings may not be realistic, but it is realistic to take steps to stop these emotions from becoming so strong or persistent that they are hazardous to our mental or physical health, relationships, or work.

The types of unhelpful thoughts that Louisa first had illustrate some common patterns in "either-or," "all-or-nothing" thinking. As Louisa recognized, these common unhelpful patterns of thinking included "catastrophizing," "shoulding," overgeneralizing, using selective attention, and labeling. These concepts are summarized in Display 4.3.

Applying the ABCs of Thinking and Feeling to Your Situation

It takes practice to use the ABCs of Thinking and Feeling as well as Louisa did. Many ways of thinking that make us overly upset (e.g., unconstructively angry, depressed) are habits that have developed over years. The following steps can help you learn to manage your stressful reactions to the difficult situations you face during your work in a nursing home.

Make multiple photocopies of the ABCs of Thinking and Feeling Form in the appendix. Then, at the end of a work day, think of one time when you were upset or stressed. Using one copy of the form, record how you felt (i.e., the emotional consequences) in the "C" column.

Go to column "A" and record what happened that got you upset or stressed (i.e., the activating event). Then go to the column marked "B" and record your thoughts or beliefs about the event. Notice whether you were thinking in an either-or, all-or-nothing way. See if you were catastrophizing, shoulding, overgeneralizing, using selective attention, or labeling.

Each day for a week, consider something that stressed or upset you that day and complete an ABCs of Thinking and Feeling Form. During this week, do not fill in the "D" column for disputing thoughts and feelings.

At the end of the week, look at each form and review the things you thought (i.e., your self-talk) about each activating event. Then question those thoughts. It may not be necessary to dispute some of the thoughts. Thoughts about how you would have preferred something to happen or thoughts about how what happened was unfortunate may be quite reasonable. These kinds of thoughts accompany periods of mild to moderate unpleasant feelings such as disappointment, regret, annoyance, or sadness. Such periodic, less intense feelings are not problematic for

Either-Or, All-or-Nothing Thinking

When we think in either-or, all-or-nothing ways, we see ourselves, others, or situations in extremes. For example, either-or, all-or-nothing thinking might cause us to see ourselves, someone else, or something else as completely helpful or completely useless—rather than partly or sometimes helpful.

Common Patterns of Thinking that Can Lead to Either-Or, All-Or-Nothing Thinking

Catastrophizing is seeing things as worse than they are. Clues that we are catastrophizing include describing an event that may be unfortunate as terrible, horrible, or awful, even though limited or no harm or damage has been done.

Shoulding is believing that something must be, needs to be, or has to be a certain way. When we engage in this type of thinking and circumstances are not as we believe they should be, we are likely to feel very frustrated, angry, depressed, confused, or anxious.

Overgeneralizing is believing that something we have done, seen, or experienced once, occasionally, or even often, happens much more than it actually does or "all of the time."

Using Selective Attention involves seeing only certain things while ignoring others. This is like using a "mental filter," filtering some things out of our awareness. When we see only negative things and filter out positive things, we are using selective attention.

Labeling is categorically describing people (including ourselves) or things in certain ways because of some of their behaviors or characteristics. When we say that a person is bad because he or she did a bad thing, we are labeling.

Caring for People with Challenging Behaviors: Essential Skills and Successful Strategies in Long-Term Care

health, relationships, or work. The goal of using the ABCs of Thinking and Feeling is not to eliminate all unpleasant emotional experiences. Rather, the goal is to prevent upset feelings and stress from becoming so great that they are unconstructive, damaging, or harmful.

To complete the "D" section on a form—that is, to dispute the beliefs, thoughts, or self-talk listed in the "B" section—ask yourself, "What evidence supports what I think or believe about what happened?" Another helpful question is, "Are there other explanations, possibilities, or ways to think about what happened?" Again, pay particular attention to either-or, all-or-nothing thinking. It is important to notice and dispute catastrophizing, shoulding, overgeneralizing, using selective attention, and labeling.

Repeat this process each week, and continue using it until you notice improvement in how you usually feel or until you are better addressing periodic difficult feelings. With this kind of practice, you may notice that you are less likely to engage in either-or, all-or-nothing thinking or to rely as heavily on unhelpful, stress-promoting ways of thinking. After a while, such formal practice may become unnecessary. If you stop practicing and notice that you are having more intense difficult feelings, begin again, using Display 4.4 as a reference. For preliminary practice with the ABCs of Thinking and Feeling, try Exercise 4.1.

USING OUR FEELINGS TO UNCOVER THE MOTIVATIONS FOR RESIDENT BEHAVIORS

Again, the goal of using the ABCs of Thinking and Feeling is to keep our feelings from harming our overall well-being, not to eliminate feelings. In fact, we can use our feelings, even unpleasant ones, constructively. In our work with nursing home residents, we can use our emotional reactions as clues to how best to react to residents' difficult behavior. Residents' challenging behaviors share some common motivations, and there are common caregiver reactions to these behaviors. By recognizing our feelings, we can make an educated guess about why a resident is behaving in a certain way.

The Need for Attention

We all have the need for attention, the need to feel connected to others, and the need to feel that we matter. The desire for attention is frequently related to wanting to be recognized, respected, valued, and considered important. A common motivation for difficult resident behavior is the desire for attention. When a resident has a strong need for attention, he or she may use the call bell often or have many questions or complaints that are never resolved in what the resident considers a satisfactory manner. The resident may be very "chatty" as well.

Reactions to Attention-Seeking Behavior   Annoyance is a common caregiver reaction to attention-seeking behavior. A caregiver's feeling of annoyance can be a clue that the resident is really trying to meet the need for attention. Unfortunately,

Disputing Unhelpful Thoughts or Beliefs

When you are stressed or upset, notice your thoughts concerning the events about which you are stressed or upset. Then ask, "What evidence supports what I think or believe about what happened? Are there other explanations, possibilities, or ways to think about what happened?" Answers to these questions can be used to dispute unhelpful thoughts.

Question and dispute either-or, all-or-nothing thinking. Question and dispute ways of thinking — such as catastrophizing, shoulding, overgeneralizing, using selective attention, and labeling — that can cause or contribute to an either-or, all-or-nothing point of view. The following questions are suggested for each type of thinking.

Catastrophizing Is what happened really horrible, terrible, or awful? How bad was the harm or damage that was done? If there was harm or damage, can it be repaired? Would it be more accurate to say that what happened was unfortunate rather than a catastrophe?

Shoulding Is it really true that what I am thinking is what should or must be? Won't something happen if it *must* happen? Isn't it true that expecting or demanding that reality be something other than what it is will only frustrate, anger, sadden, or disappoint me? Isn't it true that insisting that things must or should happen is holding myself and others to an unrealistic standard? Wouldn't it be more realistic to think that these are circumstances that I prefer rather than what must be?

Overgeneralizing Is it really true that what I am upset about always happens? Does it ever *not* happen? Is it possible that if I watch carefully, I will see times when it does not happen?

Using Selective Attention Is it really true that nothing positive happens (or that this person — or I — never do anything positive)? Is it possible that if I watch carefully, I will see positive things? Is it possible that I have been overlooking positive things?

Labeling Is it true that this person is (or that I am) completely, unchangeably _____ (fill in the blank with any unhelpful label — e.g., lazy, mean, incompetent, racist, sexist)? Isn't it true that people's behavior can change? Do I behave exactly the same way that I did 10 years ago? Does anyone behave in exactly the same way in all situations across his or her whole life?

Caring for People with Challenging Behaviors: Essential Skills and Successful Strategies in Long-Term Care
© 2005 Stephen Weber Long. Published by Health Professions Press, Inc. (http://www.healthpropress.com).
All rights reserved.

Exercise 4.1

Think about an incident in which a nursing home resident behaved in a difficult manner about which you felt angry, depressed, or stressed. If you cannot think of such an incident involving a resident, think of one in which someone else behaved in a way to which you had a very strong negative emotional or stress reaction. Complete the ABCD box below for the incident.

First, under "C," record how you felt about what the person did.

Next, under "A," record the difficult behavior—the activating event. Be specific. For example, rather than writing, "Mr. X refused care," it would be better to say how he did this—perhaps "Mr. X tried to kick me when I approached to help him out of bed."

Then, under "B," record your thoughts or beliefs about the activating event when you had your very strong negative emotional or stress reaction. Again, be specific. For example, you might have had thoughts such as, "He can't [shouldn't, must not] do that!" "He always does things like this!" "He is just a violent person!" and "He kicks or hits everyone!"

Finally, under "D," record ideas that dispute the thoughts you listed under "B." Ask yourself questions such as, "Isn't it true that if something can't, shouldn't, or must not happen, it doesn't?" "Isn't it true that insisting that something that does happen can't, shouldn't, or must not is demanding that reality be something it is not?" "Is it true that he *always* does this?" "Aren't there any times he doesn't?" "Is it true that he is nothing but violent?" and "Isn't there anyone he doesn't kick?"

A **Activating event**	B **Beliefs**	C **Emotional consequence**	D **Dispute beliefs**

it is also fairly common for us as caregivers to respond according to our annoyance rather than according to the need being expressed by the resident.

When we respond out of annoyance, we may behave in ways that do not address the need motivating the resident's behavior. We may, for example, avoid the resident. However, because the resident will likely require true assistance at some time, we will have to respond eventually. In fact, ignoring a resident usually reinforces his or her need for attention. Furthermore, it likely reinforces the resident's belief that getting needed attention requires persistent attention-seeking behavior.

A caregiver who feels guilty about being annoyed may constantly go to a resident in response to difficult attention-seeking behavior without a real plan to address the need in a way that will reduce the problem behavior. This caregiver response also tends to reinforce the difficult behavior.

Using Our Emotional Reactions to Attention-Seeking Behavior   When we use our annoyance as information about what the resident needs, we can recognize that the desire for attention is a legitimate need. The resident may be expressing it in a difficult way, but helping him or her satisfy the need can reduce the difficult behaviors motivated by it. Our plan of action can be to provide attention, making sure to provide it especially when the resident is behaving in ways that are cooperative, helpful, and expressions of appropriate levels of independence—or at least in ways that are not problematic. By consistently providing attention at such times, we reinforce behavior that is not difficult. In cases of attention-seeking behavior that are significant problems, the stretching method described in Chapter 3 may be very helpful. In all cases of attention-seeking behavior, active listening can be a central part of providing the attention needed.

The Need for Power

A second common motivation for difficult behavior is the need for power. This need is frequently related to wanting to have a say in what is happening, to have an impact on others, to be able to do things, to be able to make decisions, and to have choices. Each person has a need for power, a need to affect other people and the course of our lives. When a resident has a strong need for power, he or she may make demands rather than requests and insist that things be done in specific ways, at specific times, by specific people.

Reactions to Power-Seeking Behavior   Anger is a common caregiver reaction to the controlling, demanding behavior motivated by a resident's need for power. A caregiver's anger at a resident can be a clue that the resident is trying to meet the need for power. It is fairly common, though, for caregivers to respond out of the anger rather than to the need being expressed by the resident's behavior.

A problem with responding out of anger is that it usually does not meet the need that motivated the difficult behavior. We may, for example, persist in or increase our attempts to stay in charge. Yet, this response will almost certainly reinforce the resident's need for personal power. Difficult behavior motivated by this need will then be more likely to continue or get worse as we engage in such power struggles.

Using Our Emotional Reactions to Power-Seeking Behavior   When we use our angry feelings as information, we can recognize that the resident's behavior may reflect the need for power—that is, the resident's need to have an effect on or a say in what is happening. The resident might be expressing the need in a difficult way, but effectively helping him or her satisfy the need can reduce the problem behavior. We can help by regularly providing numerous opportunities for the resident to have a say in the things we do with the resident, including things from routine care, to room assignments, to—in some instances—developing nursing home policies.

The Desire for Revenge

Revenge is a third motivation for difficult behavior. We all need to receive responsive attention from others—that is, to see that what matters to us has an effect on those around us. When we feel that we are being neglected or made powerless, we may react by increasing attempts to get attention and exert power. If what we do does not get us attention and a sense of power, we may try to hurt those we deem responsible for the hurt we feel. We may try to make those people feel insignificant. When we are particularly vulnerable or dependent, being neglected and powerless can be very frightening. However, we often will struggle against fear by getting the attention and sense of power that hurting others can bring.

When a nursing home resident believes that attempts to get needed attention and validation of personal worth and power have persistently failed, he or she may behave in very difficult ways. For example, the resident may curse and insult caregivers about their intelligence, job position, race, ethnicity, or gender. Residents with severe impairments in the ability to think clearly or who are extremely stressed by their circumstances or life history may even try to hit staff members or hurt them in other physical ways.

Reactions to Revenge-Seeking Behavior   Caregivers often become furious in response to residents' hostile language or behavior. Such a feeling can be a clue that the resident's ability to tolerate feeling neglected or overpowered is severely overwhelmed. It is not unusual, though, for caregivers to react in anger over being attacked. For example, the staff member may angrily scold, reprimand, threaten, or insult the resident. The staff member may also increase attempts to subdue, overpower, or control the resident. This is the approach of "I'll show you," "You won't get away with that," or "I'll give you a dose of your own medicine." When caregivers take this approach, they do not usually recognize that it often is based in their own desire for revenge. A significant problem with this approach is that it frequently reinforces a resident's sense of being hurt, wronged, or mistreated. It tends to make hostile, aggressive behavior that is motivated by the desire for revenge more likely.

Using Our Reactions to Revenge-Seeking Behavior   Feeling furious with a resident can be a strong clue that the resident's behavior may be motivated by the desire for revenge—that the resident feels overpowered and neglected. By tuning in to the resident and responding to his or her underlying needs, we may reduce the resident's problem behaviors that are motivated by vengeful feelings. Using active listening skills and the techniques for encouraging positive behavior can help a resident feel that we are paying attention and are responsive to his or her needs.

It is important to consider that in an escalating problem situation, someone may become violent. It is not permissible for a staff member to intentionally harm a resident (e.g., by using undue force to coerce compliance) or allow him or her to be harmed (e.g., by looking the other way during an escalating situation between agitated individuals). At the same time, it is important to take steps to avoid being physically hurt by a resident (see Display 4.5).

Inadequacy

A fourth frequent motivation for challenging behavior among residents is the feeling of inadequacy. This feeling can be related to a sense that it is useless to keep trying. A resident may believe that he or she has no worth, no effect on what is happening, and no significance to anyone. Resident behaviors motivated by this feeling include withdrawal, isolation, and doing little or nothing to care for oneself.

Reactions to Displays of Inadequacy   Caregivers commonly respond to a resident's displays of inadequacy by feeling hopeless and helpless in their work with that person. They may come to see the resident as being incapable. Caregivers may stop encouraging the person to engage in activities, including small steps in daily routines. Some staff members avoid the resident to avoid feeling useless.

Responding out of feelings of futility, hopelessness, or helplessness will not help the resident's underlying need for attention and a sense of power or competence, which are fostered by relationships with other people. Not expecting or encouraging a resident to do even small things can reinforce his or her feeling of inadequacy. Having little interaction with the resident can make him or her feel a lack of connection with others. Connection can go a long way in helping a person feel that needed attention is being received. It can help a resident believe that he or she matters, is significant, and has an impact on others—all of which provide a sense of personal power and adequacy.

Using Our Emotional Reactions to Displays of Inadequacy   Our feelings of futility, hopelessness, or helplessness in dealing with a resident can be clues that the resident has given up. Our goal can then be a step-by-step increase in our expectations of what the resident can do, being mindful of obstacles to overcome and supporting and encouraging effort and success. See Displays 4.6 and 4.7 for summaries of the concepts explored in this section. Exercise 4.2 gives you an opportunity to enhance your understanding.

Avoiding Physical Harm by a Resident

1. **Be alert** to any signs that the resident is getting agitated. These signs can include making threats or threatening gestures, yelling, engaging in intense staring, or making repeated loud demands.

2. **Back off** when the resident becomes loud or insulting, physically resists, or tries to hurt you — as long as the resident and others are not at immediate risk of harm.

3. **Use good listening skills,** restating what you hear the resident say. Allow the resident to make choices about what will happen next. It might be good to offer limited choices such as, "Would you like me to help you now, or would it be better for me to leave?" (as long as your leaving does not put anyone at immediate risk of harm). Or you might say something such as, "I will be glad to help you now. But if you shout at me again, I'll know you've chosen for me to leave and come back later." With very confused and agitated residents, it may be more helpful to use a calm tone of voice and describe what you are going to do as you guide and assist the resident. Compliment, praise, or acknowledge positive behavior or improvements in behavior by making comments such as, "Thanks for talking to me about the problem. That helps me know what I can do to help."

4. **If the resident calms down,** continue using good listening skills and other techniques for encouraging positive behavior as you provide care. If the resident does not become calm enough, leave him or her alone and try to provide needed care later, as long as that does not put anyone at risk of immediate harm.

5. **If the difficult behavior continues** when you try to offer care later, consider getting another staff member — one with whom the resident usually gets along — to stand in for you.

6. **Have two caregivers provide care,** if applicable. This is particularly useful with residents who are severely confused or overwhelmed. The caregivers can work as a team to distract the resident from triggers for agitation as they use active listening skills and techniques for encouraging positive behavior. Having two caregivers can improve care and safety when it is necessary to provide close supervision and guidance for very confused and easily agitated residents' movements when they are assisted with things such as activities of daily living.

7. **If a resident's behavior becomes an immediate, significant threat** to anyone's well-being — including your own — follow your nursing home's policy for crisis management.

Caring for People with Challenging Behaviors: Essential Skills and Successful Strategies in Long-Term Care

Common Motivations for Residents' Difficult Behavior

Attention: Many difficult behaviors are motivated by residents' needs for attention.

Power: Residents sometimes engage in challenging behavior when they are trying to exert power over what is happening to or around them.

Revenge: Revenge involves the desire to hurt others or a particular person. It comes from the belief that others have, or the particular person has, hurt the individual. This a common motivation for many resident behaviors described as hostile, aggressive, insulting, abusive, or violent.

Feelings of inadequacy: When a nursing home resident feels inadequate or hopeless, he or she will not do many things effectively. In some cases, the resident will not even try.

Source: Dinkmeyer, McKay, McKay, & Dinkmeyer (1998).

Common Caregiver Reactions to Residents' Difficult Behavior

When the resident's difficult behavior is motivated by	Caregivers often feel	And caregivers often respond by
A need for attention	Annoyed	Avoiding or withdrawing from the resident
A need for power	Angry	Insisting on being in charge
A desire for revenge	Furious	Taking the approach of "I'll show you," "You won't get away with that," or "I'll give you a dose of your own medicine"
		Scolding
		Reprimanding
A sense of inadequacy	Hopeless	Expecting the resident to do very little, if anything

These common motivations for difficult behavior are ways of being involved, of being connected and attached to others. They are ways of belonging. If a resident cannot find relationships or does not know how to foster them in positive ways, he or she will likely engage in challenging behavior.

Applying good listening skills and techniques for encouraging positive behavior (e.g., using praise, compliments, and acknowledgment; allowing choices)—instead of replying in the ways listed above—can help meet residents' attachment needs and decrease the difficult things they may do to belong.

Source: Dinkmeyer, McKay, McKay, & Dinkmeyer (1998).

Exercise 4.2

Think of an incident in which a nursing home resident behaved in a way about which you felt annoyed, angry, or helpless. If you cannot think of one involving a nursing home resident, think of one involving someone else.

Briefly describe the incident.

Briefly describe the following:

1. What need, desire, or feeling (e.g., the need for attention or power, the desire for revenge, or feelings of inadequacy) motivated the person's difficult behavior

2. What you did or could have done to address the need, desire, or feeling that motivated the difficult behavior

BREATHING-FOCUSED RELAXATION

In addition to the previously described stress management techniques, a helpful relaxation technique focuses simply on breathing. Like progressive muscle relaxation or mental imagery, breathing-focused relaxation can be used in conjunction with other techniques or by itself. For instance, you can use it to deepen and continue your relaxation following progressive muscle relaxation or mental imagery, or it can be used alone during the 10–20 minutes you set aside each day for practicing relaxation.

First, think of a simple word or phrase such as "Calm," "Peace," "One," or "I'm becoming more deeply relaxed." Pick a word or phrase that you like—one that has meaning to you and that you associate with contentment and relaxation. It will be your special word or phrase.

Sit or lie comfortably with your eyes closed. Breathe naturally, in and out. Just focus on your breathing. There is no need to make any special effort, just breathe. Each time you breathe out, say your special word or phrase. For example, breathe in and then as you exhale, say, "One." Whether you say it aloud or to yourself is up to you.

As you continue focusing on breathing and repeating your word or phrase, other thoughts may enter your mind. When you notice this, return your attention to breathing and repeating your word or phrase each time you exhale. See Display 4.8 for a summary of this relaxation technique.

PRACTICING TECHNIQUES OUTSIDE OF RELAXATION SESSIONS

To get the greatest benefit from relaxation techniques, it is very helpful to practice regularly, 10–20 minutes each day. Frequently, such practice allows people to achieve deep levels of relaxation and to turn on their body's relaxation response at times other than practice sessions.

Following approximately a week of regular practice, try using your ability to relax in other situations. Keep your regular practice sessions, but add mini sessions by using parts of the relaxation methods at different times of the day. For example, after finishing your work with a resident, stop to take a deep breath, inhaling as you slowly count to 5. Then, exhale just as slowly and count to 10. Repeating this three times in a row can help you counteract some of the stress of your work.

Another mini session you might try is noticing where your body is most tense, such as your upper back, neck, or jaw. Wherever the muscles are most tense, let the tension go. Feel those muscles loosen and relax. You can do this at any time of the day—before working with a resident who engages in challenging behavior, while walking down the hall, or during a break.

You may even focus on your breathing as it happens naturally, repeating your special word or phrase each time you exhale. You can try this for a few moments as you sit down to lunch, for instance.

It is a good idea to experiment with the different relaxation methods during the day to find how they can help you. Remember, though, to continue your regu-

Breathing-Focused Relaxation

Practicing relaxation techniques for 10–20 minutes per day can help you manage the effects of stress. Breathing-focused relaxation can be used alone or with other relaxation methods. As with other relaxation techniques, the goal is to get as relaxed as possible without falling asleep. You can use breathing-focused relaxation to continue or deepen your relaxation by following these steps:

1. **Choose a special word or phrase** such as "Calm," "Peace," "One," or "I am getting more deeply relaxed." Pick a word or phrase that you associate with contentment and relaxation.

2. **Sit or lie comfortably** in a place where you will be undisturbed for 10–20 minutes. Close your eyes and breathe naturally.

3. **Each time you exhale, say your special word or phrase.** You can say this aloud or silently—whatever works best for you.

4. **When other thoughts come into your mind,** return your focus to breathing and saying your word or phrase as you exhale.

Caring for People with Challenging Behaviors: Essential Skills and Successful Strategies in Long-Term Care

lar daily sessions in a comfortable place where you are free from distractions. Setting aside this time may seem difficult, so give yourself credit for what you do (even if it is less than 10 minutes) and simply set a goal of gradually increasing the amount of time you spend in practice. It is best not to get stressed out about trying to relax!

SUMMARY

Chapter 4 covered how thinking and feeling are linked to the stress of working with nursing home residents who behave in difficult ways. The chapter looked at two methods of using thoughts and feelings to manage stress. First, the ABCs of Thinking and Feeling can help us to see how our thoughts about an event affect how we feel. By disputing unhelpful, stress-promoting thoughts, we can reduce our stress level. Second, our feelings can give clues to what is motivating the resident's actions. Using an educated guess about what is motivating the behavior, we can take steps to help the resident meet the need underlying the behavior. Doing this can be very effective in reducing or eliminating problem behaviors. This chapter also discussed breathing-focused relaxation and the importance of practicing relaxation techniques throughout the day.

Obstacles to Using Effective Techniques

This chapter looks at obstacles to addressing nursing home residents' problem behaviors in the most effective ways. Obstacles to using the techniques described in this book can take three forms: personal, institutional, and societal. Personally, we may not know about or be familiar enough with the techniques. Institutionally, the policies or usual practices of a nursing home may interfere with providing attention to the needs underlying residents' problem behaviors. Finally, a society that tends to undervalue people who are older or ill will not devote the time, money, or other resources to meet their needs.

Chapter 5 ends by describing how good relationships with others can help us cope with stress. It presents ways of improving our interactions and relationships with others that can help us manage stress.

PERSONAL OBSTACLES

We may not know about or practice the techniques or skills that are most likely to ameliorate challenging behavior. We may also have set ideas about ourselves and others that do not help us use the best approaches to difficult situations with residents. The following beliefs serve as examples:

- A person's behavior should change if you tell him or her that the behavior is unacceptable.

- Using only negative consequences will teach someone to stop a problematic behavior.

- Some behaviors are just plain bad, and anyone who engages in them does not deserve respect.

- Trying to understand challenging behavior is just making excuses for the behavior and blaming others.

- Nothing that one person does affects the way another person thinks, feels, or behaves—especially if that person has a mental illness, dementia, or a difficult personality.

- Some people do things for no reason.

- Someone who does bad things is just a bad person.

- People do not change.

Another group of beliefs that are likely to impede developing our skills is related to responsibility, authority, and power. Some of these beliefs include:

- It is not my job or responsibility to deal with a resident's difficult behavior.

- A resident should be made to stop behaving in insulting, verbally abusive, or threatening ways.

- It is the responsibility of those in authority to make people stop engaging in challenging behavior.

Coping with Our Personal Obstacles

A first step toward dealing with obstacles that we put in our own way is to recognize the possibility of doing this. A strong clue is that the difficult behavior of the resident in question never seems to change or gets worse. While it is important to address medical conditions contributing to the problem, lack of behavioral improvement is a sign that we may need more training or supervision in the techniques described in this book. Consulting with a qualified mental health professional, taking classes, studying, and getting supervision can help. Generations of mental health professionals have found that their own participation in personal psychotherapy greatly assists the effectiveness of their work. It may be a big help to anyone who works in a nursing home, too. Psychotherapy typically entails meeting with a psychotherapist on at least a weekly basis. In addition to being effective treatment for depression and anxiety, it can help with substance abuse, family and relationship problems, and specifically with work-related difficulties. Psychotherapy can be a useful tool in helping us better recognize and respond to our own needs and those of others.

Consultation with a mental health professional about a particular resident's problem behavior will probably result in the recommendation to use methods similar to those presented in this book and in some suggestions about how to use them more effectively. It is not likely that the mental health professional will take responsibility for making the resident behave well. Successfully addressing a resident's problem behavior requires the efforts of each person who works with him or her.

It is not usually helpful to insist that a person in authority make a resident's challenging behavior stop. Relying on force, intimidation, threats, restraints, or negative consequences does not promote emotional or physical health or improved behavior among residents.

Primarily authoritarian approaches to behavior problems do not encourage exercising, maintaining, or developing a resident's sense of competence, self-control, or self-worth. Such approaches do encourage the resident's experience of frustration, resentment, anger, and depression—all of which can motivate additional problem behaviors.

Behavior problems are signs of psychological distress. Consultants, supervisors, and administrators have important roles in making the nursing home an environment that promotes residents' general well-being—including their psychological well-being. However, it is the responsibility of everyone working in the nursing home to play a role in this, too. It really *is* part of the job—a big part. Display 5.1 summarizes personal obstacles.

INSTITUTIONAL OBSTACLES

Supervisors and administrators are very influential in how the nursing home as an institution operates. The policies and procedures that they support affect the facility's values and goals. Their style of leadership also has a significant impact on what others in the nursing home do.

Nursing homes commonly emphasize certain things that make it difficult for staff to use the most effective techniques for dealing with residents' behavior problems. An overemphasis on the physical and medical tasks and interventions performed by staff can overshadow the psychological tasks and interventions needed for a healthy nursing home environment. Clearly, it is very important to ensure that residents get needed medications, are clean, have clean bedding and clothes, and are fed. However, an exclusive or even primary focus on these tasks—and not a fundamental emphasis on the interactions with residents during and after such tasks—can lead to significant behavior and overall health problems, even if physical and medical needs are met. Problems arise when factors that make interactions positive are considered unnecessary or outside of what staff are paid to do—especially if these things require more time and effort than staff, managers, or administrators think they should.

Another institutional emphasis that can cause problems is the use of minimal resources—that is, minimal numbers of qualified staff to accomplish the "real" physical tasks. Not having a workable approach to retaining staff is also a frequent problem. Working well in a nursing home involves complex interpersonal, organizational, and task skills—many of which develop largely through experience and training. High staff turnover prevents this from happening.

Working on Personal Obstacles to Using Effective Approaches to Residents' Difficult Behaviors

Personal obstacles can impede using the best techniques for dealing with residents' problem behaviors. We can do the following to address this issue:

Recognize that if medical conditions have been addressed and there still is no improvement or a behavior gets worse, a significant part of the problem may be your lack of knowledge or skill regarding effective techniques for addressing problem behavior.

Consult with a qualified mental health professional, attend classes on dealing with nursing home residents' psychological needs and difficult behaviors, and/or get supervision on these topics. Generations of mental health professionals have found that their own participation in personal psychotherapy greatly assists the effectiveness of their work. It would likely be helpful for those working in nursing homes as well. It can help address difficulties we have in our work and our relationships. Psychotherapy is an effective treatment for things such as depression, anxiety, and substance abuse. It can help us better recognize our own and others' needs and how best to respond to them.

Understand that difficult behaviors are signs of psychological distress. Each person working in a nursing home shares responsibility for meeting residents' needs, including the psychological needs that can motivate problem behavior. These needs can be met by practicing the basic techniques of addressing behavior problems.

Caring for People with Challenging Behaviors: Essential Skills and Successful Strategies in Long-Term Care
© 2005 Stephen Weber Long. Published by Health Professions Press, Inc. (http://www.healthpropress.com).
All rights reserved.

Leadership style in a nursing home can also affect how well nursing home residents' problem behaviors are addressed. A primarily "top-down" approach relies on telling staff what to do rather than helping them develop skills they can use responsibly and creatively. This approach relies on orders being given and emphasizes doing things to avoid negative consequences from authority figures. It focuses staff attention on the power of supervisors rather than on flexible and creative ways to address the challenges of their work.

Addressing Institutional Obstacles

Job descriptions for all nursing home personnel must clearly state that addressing the mental health, behavioral, or psychological needs of nursing home residents is a central part of each job position. New employee orientation can underscore this crucial aspect of work in a nursing home. Another critical element of appropriate job descriptions is outlining staff members' responsibilities for participating in ongoing training and supervision aimed at working with residents' behavior problems or psychological needs. Supervisors and administrators can support staff members' use of effective approaches by modeling their use with residents. Because the techniques apply in situations and relationships beyond those involving residents, supervisors and administrators can model the use of the techniques with staff members as well. Continuing education and supervision, including peer supervision, in the use and promotion of these techniques and related matters are essential for supervisors and administrators. Peer supervision might take the form of groups of supervisors or administrators meeting to discuss issues related to their work on addressing the challenging behaviors of residents.

Those who facilitate the development of a nursing home's policies and practices also have the task of ensuring that ongoing training and supervision are available. It is important to recognize that training and supervision sessions are not helpful when staff cannot get away from direct patient care. Scheduling policies can give staff time to attend training sessions, to focus during supervision sessions, and to use the techniques described in this book.

It also is not helpful to train staff in techniques that are difficult to practice because of work-load demands. In some instances, it may be necessary to reassess standards used to determine adequate numbers of staff. For example, it may not be realistic to expect a nursing assistant who helps 13 or more residents with most activities of daily living to be readily available for training and supervision or to be able to carry out the best practices for addressing residents' psychological, behavioral, or mental health needs.

Guidelines for staffing or consultation by other disciplines and occupations are also critical. Recreational therapists, psychologists, psychiatrists and other medical staff, social workers, rehabilitation staff, housekeepers, clerical staff, dietary personnel, and clergy all contribute to the optimal functioning of a nursing home. Each of these disciplines and occupations focuses on critical aspects of the well-being of residents, aspects for which any one discipline (e.g., nursing) cannot reasonably be made fully responsible.

Attending to adequate staffing and consultation can enhance job satisfaction among staff and help reduce staff turnover. Another thing that helps retain staff is a democratic style of leadership. This approach encourages staff to develop their abilities to work both creatively and cooperatively, generating solutions to challenges and working together toward a shared mission. With this type of leadership, the mission of the nursing home emphasizes creating an environment—through relationships with residents—that is sensitive and responsive to residents' physical, psychological, and other needs. Enhancing staff members' roles depends on supervisors and administrators being open to insights and feedback from all staff. It calls for leadership in facilitating the process of shared decision making and in implementing resulting decisions that are consistent with the nursing home's mission.

The democratic style of leadership values each person, as well as his or her capacities and contributions. This style of leadership is very different from the authoritarian style described previously. The authoritarian style may have short-term benefits: staff may do what they are told, when they are told to do it, and how they are told to do it. Typically, though, staff under this type of leadership will do little else. They tend to be less creative in solving the many challenges that confront them when the leader is not present or for which the leader has not left specific orders. In addition, groups with authoritarian leaders are prone to unconstructive conflict, arguing, and fighting.

A third type of leadership is the laissez-faire approach. Supervisors and administrators who use this hands-off style avoid providing guidance and facilitating processes aimed at addressing challenges or accomplishing goals. Instead, they leave staff members on their own. Unfortunately, this style usually leads to very little being accomplished. It is not likely to address residents' difficult behavior or psychological needs.

To address the institutional obstacles that come from authoritarian or laissez-faire leadership styles, supervisors and administrators can work on developing more democratic leadership skills. Ongoing team-building processes and programs can be very helpful. Team building requires open communication (promoted by good listening skills), acknowledgment of the important roles and contributions of team members (promoted by praise and compliments), respect for each person's independent work (promoted by allowing choices), cooperative problem solving (based on understanding that problems have triggers and, if they continue, have reinforcers), and a sense of a shared mission (providing for the needs of nursing home residents). These points illustrate that integrating this book's basic techniques into a nursing home's day-to-day routines with residents and among staff constitutes a significant step in the process of team-building. See Display 5.2 for a review of ways to address institutional obstacles.

SOCIETAL OBSTACLES

A nursing home's functioning is also related to the wider society. Society's general attitudes about nursing homes affect whether a nursing home's services are valued. Widely held opinions, beliefs, and feelings about aging, elderly people, dis-

Working on Institutional Obstacles to Using Effective Approaches to Residents' Difficult Behaviors

Institutional obstacles are the policies or practices of a nursing home that limit using the basic techniques for addressing residents' problem behaviors. Nursing home supervisors and administrators can work on such obstacles by applying these guidelines:

Helpful job descriptions for all nursing home personnel clearly state that providing care for residents' mental health and behavioral or psychological needs is a central part of each position. They state the expectation that all staff members will develop proficiency in the basic techniques of meeting the psychological needs of residents and of dealing with difficult behavior.

New employee orientation can provide an overview of recognizing signs of psychological distress—behavior problems, for example—and the basic techniques for dealing with them.

Because the basic techniques are descriptions of interpersonal skills, they are helpful in any relationship. **Supervisors and administrators can model the use of these skills** in dealings with others, including staff and residents.

Ongoing training and supervision in the use of basic techniques is important for all staff, supervisors, and administrators.

Staff members need enough time away from direct patient care to regularly attend training and supervision sessions, so appropriate scheduling and staffing policies are necessary. Having adequate numbers of staff also ensures that one's workload does not make using the basic techniques too difficult.

Cultivate a leadership style that values each person's contributions—a style that helps others develop skills and encourages the creative and cooperative use of those skills. This democratic leadership style promotes open communication and responds to feedback and suggestions that will help the nursing home fulfill its mission. This style facilitates a team approach to accomplishing an organization's goals.

Keep the nursing home's primary mission in mind: to provide an environment—through relationships with residents—that is sensitive and responsive to residents' physical, psychological, and other needs.

Caring for People with Challenging Behaviors: Essential Skills and Successful Strategies in Long-Term Care
© 2005 Stephen Weber Long. Published by Health Professions Press, Inc. (http://www.healthpropress.com).
All rights reserved.

abilities, disease, and death influence the amount of attention and resources society devotes to nursing homes.

Our society tends to value youth over age. There are widespread negative beliefs about aging. Examples include the belief that people's personalities change in negative ways as they age and that all older people are depressed. In fact, negative changes in personality and major depression are the exception among older people. Though depression is more common among nursing home residents than among older people in the wider community, depression can be treated successfully in nursing homes with adequate resources.

Responding to Societal Obstacles

People and things with which we become familiar are often less likely to frighten us. Getting to know about them can help us confront and work through our negative perceptions and fears. A nursing home can help the broader society to confront and better cope with its negative perceptions and fears of aging, elderly people, disabilities, disease, and death by strengthening ties that promote familiarity with the nursing home world. A nursing home can develop and deepen relationships with religious and volunteer or service organizations as well as educational institutions—from child care centers to graduate and professional schools. The aim is to deepen and broaden connections between the people of the nursing home and those of other organizations.

A nursing home can sponsor entertainment, cultural, and educational events that are open to and involve nursing home residents and staff, members of other organizations or institutions, and the general community. Interaction and dialogue among people from these different groups can provide the nursing home with valuable feedback about how it and residents are perceived and about ways of improving those perceptions. A summary of overcoming societal obstacles appears in Display 5.3.

A SYSTEM VIEW

We as individuals, the institution of the nursing home, and the wider society together form a system. As parts of the system, the individual, the nursing home, and the society interact with and influence each other.

It may seem impossible to change institutional, social, or even individual attitudes or policies that have a negative impact on nursing home residents. However, the acts of individuals do affect the acts of others. The more positive our individual influence is in the nursing home, the better the odds are that improvements will happen within the nursing home and beyond. The techniques described in this book for addressing difficult behaviors among nursing home residents can be used to some degree in our individual dealings with everyone in the nursing home. We do not have to wait for institutional or social change to use these approaches. The more we use them, the more we will contribute to improvements.

Working on Societal Obstacles to Using Effective Approaches to Residents' Difficult Behaviors

Negative views of nursing homes and unpleasant preconceptions of elderly people—related to fears of illness, disability, and death—can undermine the broader society's support for and involvement in nursing homes. Our society's largely youthful orientation and these fears can prevent investment of enough time, money, and other resources to enable nursing homes to meet the needs of residents. Nursing homes can help members of society confront and work through negative perceptions and fears by promoting ways to become more familiar with the nursing home world. Familiarity can lead people to question their preconceptions. Some ways of encouraging this familiarity follow:

Develop and deepen relationships with religious, volunteer, or service organizations and educational institutions (from child care centers to graduate and professional schools).

Sponsor entertainment, cultural, and educational events that are open to and involve nursing home residents and staff, members of other organizations or institutions, and the community.

Look for feedback from members of the different groups that interact with the nursing home about their perceptions of the nursing home and residents and about ways of improving those perceptions.

Caring for People with Challenging Behaviors: Essential Skills and Successful Strategies in Long-Term Care
© 2005 Stephen Weber Long. Published by Health Professions Press, Inc. (http://www.healthpropress.com).
All rights reserved.

IMPROVING RELATIONSHIPS AS
A STRESS MANAGEMENT TECHNIQUE

Stressful things are a part of life. We are challenged to meet everyday demands. Our personal obstacles to coping with stress may mesh with obstacles put in place by the institutions and society of which we are a part. It can take practice to change our less constructive responses to stress. Engaging in regular exercise and using the stress management techniques described in previous chapters are good places to start. Our relationships also play an important role in managing stress.

We have examined ways of striking a better balance between the stress of everyday life and the relief of pleasant activities and relaxation. Display 1.2 in Chapter 1 lists events commonly considered pleasant; you may have noticed that many of these activities are related to being involved with other people. That is because positive interactions, or positive relationships with others, are among the most important ways of reducing stress, coping with unavoidable stress, and maintaining or improving physical and mental health. In addition to engaging in other types of pleasant activities and relaxation practice, effectively coping with stress typically includes spending time regularly with at least one other person with whom you can talk. This is someone you can talk to about yourself—about the things that happen to you (not necessarily at work), about what you think and feel. With this person, you can talk about both good and troubling things. When you talk with this person, you feel accepted, respected, and liked (or loved). This is not the kind of relationship that you have with everyone. It is a special, close relationship.

Typically, a balance between being open to others expressing themselves and expressing ourselves deepens relationships and helps us cope with stress better. Very often, mutual, give-and-take relationships are the most beneficial. These are relationships in which each person generally feels listened to, heard, and accepted. They are also relationships in which each person feels a good deal of freedom to express thoughts and feelings. Some people are better at this type of relationship than others. It may not be possible to surround yourself with only people who are good at relationships, but it is best to put limits on the number of relationships in which you give more than you get.

Relationship Skills

Much of this book deals with interactions between people—that is, interactions that form the basis of relationships. The heart of the book is about how relationships play a fundamental role in how nursing home residents, like all people, behave, think, and feel. Many of this book's techniques can be used in your relationships with people other than nursing home residents. For example, others will generally be more open to hearing what you think and feel if you regularly use active listening with them.

Another way to foster rewarding relationships is to let people know what you like about what they do. Be descriptive in praising or complimenting them. A good general rule: For every negative comment or criticism that you make, give the person at least four genuine compliments. It is good to express your appreciation for the little things, not just the big things. Examples include "I notice that you carry your neighbor's recyclables out to the curb for him. That's a very caring thing to do," or "Thanks for listening to me talk about how tough things have been at work lately. Talking it out with you helped me get some relief," or "I'm glad that you can talk to me about what's going on in your life." Notice effort, too, not just the final product—for example, "It was very good of you to try to straighten up the house before I got home."

Expressing Yourself

Each of us is likely to express some things well and others not well at all. We are also probably more skilled at expressing ourselves with some people and not with others. However, developing our ability to express ourselves well can help deepen and strengthen our relationships and general social skills. See Display 5.4 for examples of common situations in which people have difficulty expressing themselves.

Passive, Aggressive, and Assertive Communication

There are three general styles of expression: passive, aggressive, and assertive. If your usual style is passive, you typically do not say what you feel or think about what others do, or you tend to be indirect and apologetic when you do express your feelings and thoughts. An unfortunate result is that others are likely to treat you as though what you think and feel does not matter. An example of passive communication involves Jack letting his daughter Melanie borrow his car. Melanie returned the car after the time Jack needed it to get to work. When Jack got into the car, he found that the gas gauge was on empty. He did not tell Melanie that these things bothered him. In fact, when Melanie asked to borrow the car again the next day, Jack said, "Sure, it's just sitting in the driveway."

If your style is usually aggressive, you are most likely to express yourself in ways that dominate others into paying attention to you and how you see or feel about things. What you say often tells people that they are stupid or worthless for not seeing things the way you do, not treating you the way you want to be treated, or not doing the things you think they should. It tells others that what you want, feel, and think is what matters—not them. For you, it is important to come out on top in your dealings with others. Here is an example of aggressive communication using the previously presented situation: Melanie returned the car late and with nearly no gas. Jack said, "I can't believe you! You are so self-centered! Everything is about you, isn't it?! What you want. 'Gimme, gimme.' 'I want this. I want that.' You're selfish. You disgust me!"

When your style is assertive rather than aggressive or passive, you are generally able to say what you think and feel without disregarding or disrespecting yourself or others. You do not usually communicate in ways that are hurtful or humiliating. Assertiveness is most likely to build strong, beneficial relationships. Building on the same case, here is an example of assertive communication: When Melanie returned the car late with the gas gauge on empty, Jack said, "When I lent

Common Situations in Which People Have Difficulty Expressing Themselves

Turning down a person's request to borrow something of yours

Asking for expected service when it is not offered

Asking a favor of someone

Resisting sales pressure

Expressing a different opinion from the person(s) with whom you are talking

Expressing your love to someone

Asking to borrow something

Telling someone how you feel when he or she has done something unfair to you

Admitting ignorance

Turning down an invitation

Resisting an unfair demand from someone important to you

Asking for constructive criticism

Telling a friend or co-worker that something he or she says or does bothers you

Asking for clarification when you are confused

Asking a person who you do not know and who is annoying you in public to stop doing something (e.g., playing loud music on a train)

Asking if you offended someone

Telling someone that he or she disappointed you

Telling someone that you like him or her

Criticizing your spouse or partner

Complimenting someone

Source: Lewinsohn, Muñoz, Youngren, & Zeiss (1986).

Caring for People with Challenging Behaviors: Essential Skills and Successful Strategies in Long-Term Care
© 2005 Stephen Weber Long. Published by Health Professions Press, Inc. (http://www.healthpropress.com).
All rights reserved.

you my car, I got it back late and there was almost no gas in it. I felt angry because I had to get to work and I was going to be late."

Assertive communication uses "I-messages." I-messages tell what happened as you see it, how you feel about what happened, and why you feel that way. They often begin with the phrases, "What I think is . . .," " "What I feel is . . .," "The way I see the situation is. . . ." I-messages do not focus on blaming, labeling, attacking, counterattacking, threatening, telling people "You can't get away with that," humiliating people to put them in their place, or showing others who's boss.

Most people respond well to assertive communication. However, some will not; they will retreat as though attacked, perhaps acting hurt and withdrawn. Others might react with hostility to counter what seems to be an attack. When others have such negative reactions, use active listening and other ways of encouraging their positive behavior toward you. If such negative reactions are usual for someone you are obligated to live, work, or deal with, it can be good to regularly use good listening skills and other ways of supportively encouraging positive behavior.

Do not let relationships with those who frequently have strong negative reactions to your needs dominate your life. Set limits to the amount of time, energy, and effort you spend in such relationships. Setting limits can help you avoid getting overly stressed or burned out. Balance the stressful effects of these relationships by spending time with others who are more able to see, hear, and accept you. Spend some time at least once per week with someone who is able to accept you in this way. Display 5.5 reviews guidelines for assertive communication, and Exercise 5.1 presents an approach to personal application.

Setting Limits

Setting limits in a relationship means putting limits on what you are going to do for, tolerate from, invest in, or give to the other person. We set limits on what we will or will not do in response to the other person's behavior. We avoid trying to set limits on what the other person does because trying to control others does not usually lead to the best outcomes. It is generally better to encourage the person's cooperation and self-control by using the techniques described in this book.

If limit setting becomes your primary way of interacting, it is not likely to be very effective. In addition, if the setting of limits is routinely followed by rage or withdrawal and helplessness on the part of the other person, limit setting is not enough. When you are persistently setting limits or are avoiding setting any limits, you are probably in an ongoing power struggle or are feeling hopeless. In either case, you and the other person are not having your basic needs for attention, acceptance, positive regard, and control met. If these needs of yours are not filled in this relationship, it is best to have other relationships in which they are filled. If these needs are not met for someone who depends on your care, it is important to have that person's care provided by someone else until you are less stressed and are able to accept that responsibility. Limit setting can be illustrated by recasting the story of Jack and Melanie. In this scenario, Jack stated the limit by clearly

Using Assertive Communication in Relationships

Generally using assertive communication helps us effectively express ourselves to others. Using this style of communication, we clearly state what we think and feel. It can often reduce or prevent stressful interactions, may help improve difficult relationships, and may deepen and strengthen positive relationships.

Assertive communication uses I-messages to say what happened as you see it, how you feel about what happened, and why you feel that way. I-messages are not about proving who is right or wrong. When we use I-messages we do not disregard, disrespect, or apologize for our own thoughts or feelings. We simply state them.

Examples of I-messages	Examples of common, usually unhelpful alternatives (either passive or aggressive)
"When you shout at me, I feel frustrated because I want to get along with you."	"I can't stand you when you shout. If you shout again, I'll really give you something to shout about."
"You returned my car late. I felt very stressed out. I had to get to work, and I did not want to be late."	"You're such a self-centered jerk."
"I have a lot to do right now. I feel a bit over-whelmed because even though what you're asking me to do is a small thing, I don't feel like I can take on anything else just now."	"I have so much to do that I can't get everything done on time. But I'm sorry. I'll make the photo-copies you want for your meeting next week right now—just as you asked."
"You listened to me talk about what I was going through when I was having a tough time. I'm so grateful. It helped me to feel that I was not alone."	Not saying anything

Most people respond well to assertive communication, but some view it as an attack. They may react by acting hurt and withdrawing or by being hostile. When others have negative reactions to your assertive communication, use good listening skills, acknowl-edge positive things they do, and let them make choices in addressing problems. Bal-ance the stressful effects of these relationships by spending time with others who are more able to see, hear, and accept you. Spend some time at least once per week with someone who is able to accept you in this way.

Caring for People with Challenging Behaviors: Essential Skills and Successful Strategies in Long-Term Care
© 2005 Stephen Weber Long. Published by Health Professions Press, Inc. (http://www.healthpropress.com).
All rights reserved.

Exercise 5.1

Think of a time you were talking with someone at home, at work, or elsewhere and had trouble saying what you thought or felt. (See Display 5.4 for examples.) Perhaps you had trouble with speaking at all or with speaking without putting the other person down.

Briefly describe the following:

1. What happened

2. How you felt about what happened

3. Why you felt the way you did

Describe "I-messages" that you used or could have used to express yourself in this situation.

Setting Limits in Relationships

To reduce and prevent some stress, it is important to set limits on the time, energy, and effort we put into difficult interactions and relationships. We set limits by deciding what we will or will not do for, to, or with others—*not* by trying to control their behavior. Although limit setting influences the behavior of others, it is about taking care of ourselves.

Describe the limit calmly. For example, say, "If you scream at me again, I will leave the room. Then I won't talk to you again until dinner."

Act on the limit calmly. For example, say, "You just screamed at me. I see you have chosen for me to leave the room and not talk with you until dinner." Then leave the room. You could also just leave the room without saying anything.

Remember that the most effective limits are mild. They do not deprive or threaten to deprive anyone of safety, basic needs, or fundamental human rights. An example is telling a nursing home resident that if he or she insults you again, you will leave him or her safely alone for 15 minutes or find a co-worker to provide the care. Never threaten something as severe as leaving the resident confined to bed all day for insulting you.

Remember that limit setting is most effective when it is not the main focus of your dealings with anyone and when it does not result in rage or withdrawn signs of helplessness. If you are constantly setting limits—or avoiding setting any limits—you are likely in an ongoing power struggle or are feeling hopeless. Both you and the other person are not having your basic needs for attention, acceptance, positive regard, and control met. If these are not being met for you in this relationship, you need other relationships in which they are. If these needs are not being met for someone who depends on your care, see to having that person's care provided by another person until you are less stressed and are able to accept that responsibility.

Caring for People with Challenging Behaviors: Essential Skills and Successful Strategies in Long-Term Care

Exercise 5.2

Think of a time when you felt overwhelmed by what someone else wanted from you or when you felt that someone was taking advantage of you, neglecting you, or treating you disrespectfully.

Briefly describe what that person was doing.

Tell how you described or could have described the limits you would set if the troublesome treatment happened again.

Describe how you followed through or could have followed through with the limit you described.

telling Melanie that she could use the car as long as she returned it on time and with a full tank of gas. Jack told his daughter that if she brought the car back late or without a full tank of gas, he would know that Melanie chose not to be allowed to borrow his car for a week. Jack put a limit on what he would do (lend his car) and what he would tolerate (having his feelings and needs disregarded or abused). He also pointed out that Melanie had the choice of whether she would be able to borrow the car.

Melanie returned the car late but with a full tank of gas. Jack acknowledged the positive by saying it was good of her to see that the tank was full. However, he followed through with the limit of not lending his car to Melanie for a week because the car was returned late. He said, "It was good of you to fill the tank, but I see that you have chosen—by returning the car late—not to borrow the car for the next week." Melanie was angry, replying that he was unfair and ruining her plans. Jack said, "You're disappointed and angry because you can't borrow the car for a week," and left it at that.

The next time Jack lent Melanie the car, she brought it home on time and with a full tank of gas. In the future, Jack planned to continue following through with the limits he set on lending his car. Display 5.6 provides an overview of limit setting for reducing stress in relationships; Exercise 5.2 encourages personal application of this technique.

SUMMARY

Chapter 5 examined personal, institutional, and societal obstacles to using the most effective ways for addressing nursing home residents' difficult behaviors. Various suggestions were given for coping with these obstacles. We can practice recognizing the obstacles that we as individuals put in the way. Such obstacles can be overcome by getting education, training, and supervision and perhaps even psychotherapy. We also need to keep in mind that behavior problems are signs of psychological distress and that providing care for residents' psychological needs is part of the job for everyone working in the nursing home. Yet, we can recognize that a nursing home's policies and practices may impede the psychological tasks and interventions that are necessary for a healthy, safe environment. Developing and deepening relationships with organizations and institutions outside the nursing home can help address societal obstacles. Even if institutional or societal change has not occurred, it is important to use the techniques described in this book. Our individual actions can lead to improvement in a nursing home.

Chapter 5 ended by considering the importance of good relationships in managing stress. It explained how expressing ourselves well can deepen and improve relationships. In addition, the chapter described ways of limiting exposure to stress in difficult situations and relationships.

Chapter 6

Treatment Planning

The basic techniques described in *Caring for People with Challenging Behaviors* can be very useful in the treatment planning process. They can serve as a guide to some of the most effective practices in preventing and addressing nursing home residents' problem behaviors. The best treatment for behavior problems is prevention. Routine use of the basic techniques means that behavior problems are likely to be less frequent and less intense. By using these techniques as our usual ways of dealing with residents, we take a preventive approach to difficult behavior. When our attempts at prevention do not work, however, we move on to more active treatment planning.

This chapter describes two methods of treatment planning: individual and team. In the individual method, the planning is relatively informal. It occurs when an individual staff member uses the approaches described in this book to develop a therapeutic relationship with the resident—a relationship that helps to prevent or address problem behaviors. The team method is required when individual efforts need support or guidance. With the team method, the planning is formalized. It typically occurs during interdisciplinary team meetings, but the resulting approach has much in common with the individual method.

These methods of treatment planning are suggested as guides. They may be used with flexibility to account for the varying needs of different nursing homes and residents. However, if you modify these methods and do not see improved behavior, it may be best to follow the suggested methods more closely.

THE INDIVIDUAL METHOD

An individual staff member begins treatment of a resident's troubling behavior by deciding how to respond. Some behaviors are best treated by being ignored. These are infrequent behaviors or actions that are frequent but not harmful (e.g., talking to oneself, grumpiness, complaining, infrequent angry outbursts, occasional strong language). Ignoring such behaviors does not mean ignoring the needs that are motivating the behaviors. It avoids responding to the behavior by openly showing anger or annoyance, reprimanding the resident, and "educating" the resident about more appropriate behavior in the heat of the moment. Frequently, such responses reinforce the problem behavior.

Behaviors that hurt someone, emotionally or physically, are problematic. They can be harmful to the resident or to someone else. Examples are frequently shouting or screaming, persistently insulting others, making physical or verbal threats, hitting, pinching, biting, kicking, and scratching. These behaviors call for an active therapeutic approach on the part of nursing home staff. In instances when the behavior poses an immediate risk of significant harm to anyone (including the resident), follow your nursing home's policy for dealing with such situations. This may involve calling a crisis team or even the police.

With the individual approach, a realistic goal is to have a challenging behavior happen less often, be less strong, or both (see Display 6.1; see also Display 3.4). The goal could be to shorten the duration of certain behavioral episodes. Display 6.1 includes a helpful scale to measure the intensity of a difficult behavior. If a resident's problem behavior is very strong, it would be scored 5 according to the scale. In such cases, a goal could be to reduce the intensity to less than 5.

The individual method of treatment planning has five steps, and each takes approximately 2 weeks. The steps are outlined in the following sections. Each section refers to displays in *Caring for People with Challenging Behaviors* for you to review when you are at that particular step. See also Display 6.2 for a listing of the different displays for each step.

Step 1

Keep in mind that the behavior problem is likely to have both internal and external causes (Display 1.1). Step 1 involves using active listening (Display 2.1), engaging in cooperative problem solving (Display 3.6), allowing the resident to make choices (Display 2.2), using praise and other social reinforcers (Display 2.3), and containing your reactions to the resident's behavior (Displays 2.4 and 3.2). For a resident whose behavior problem involves significantly disruptive attention-seeking behavior, include the stretching techniques described in Display 3.5 as part of your initial treatment plan. Use these Step 1 techniques for the next 2 weeks.

Step 2

Assess the situation after using Step 1 for 2 weeks. If there is no improvement in the problem behavior, if it has gotten worse, or if additional improvement would be helpful, it is time for Step 2. The goal can still be to reduce the behavior's fre-

Setting Goals for Addressing Residents' Problem Behaviors

It is important to have goals in mind when trying to help a resident reduce or eliminate a problem behavior. One measurable goal might be that the behavior will happen less often than the estimated average number of times that it happens during a shift (for frequent behaviors) or during a week (for less frequent behaviors). Another goal might be to shorten episodes of the behavior. For example, if a resident typically yells for 20 minutes at a time, the goal might be that the resident will, on average, yell for less than 20 minutes. Yet another kind of goal is that the behavior will become less intense. Using the following scale, the goal might be to reduce the intensity of a behavior scored 5 to a 4 or less. Once a goal has been reached and maintained, it might be good to set a goal for further improvement.

Problem Behavior Intensity Scale

Score and intensity level	Examples
1 Very Mild	A resident tells a caregiver to go away. A resident speaks loudly or sharply but does not shout.
2 Mild	A resident periodically calls for help (without shouting) when there is no significant need for attention. A resident sometimes complains using strong language.
3 Moderate	A resident shouts but does not scream. A resident angrily shakes his or her fist at someone. A resident lightly slaps someone's hand.
4 Strong	A resident screams, perhaps using ethnic, racist, or gender slurs. A resident vigorously hits someone.
5 Very strong	A resident scratches someone, breaking that person's skin. A resident hits and bruises someone.

Displays from *Caring for People with Challenging Behaviors* to Use for Individual and Team Treatment Planning

This list presents the displays from *Caring for People with Challenging Behaviors* according to the relevant treatment planning steps.

Step 1

Display 1.1 Understanding Causes of Behavior Problems Among Nursing Home Residents

Display 2.1 Active Listening

Display 2.2 Allowing Choices

Display 2.3 Using Praise, Compliments, and Acknowledgment

Display 2.4 Things to Avoid When Trying to Encourage Positive Behavior

Display 3.2 Holding On: Dealing with Reactions to Problem Behaviors

Display 3.4 Realistic Goals for Residents' Problem Behaviors

Display 3.5 Stretching (if a resident behaves in attention-seeking ways that are very disruptive)

Display 3.6 Cooperative Problem Solving

Display 6.1 Setting Goals for Addressing Residents' Problem Behaviors

Step 2

Display 3.1 The ABCs of Behavior

Display 3.3 Determining What Triggers and Reinforces a Resident's Problem Behavior

Review the displays from Step 1.

(continued)

Display 6.2 *(continued)*

Step 3

Display 4.1 The ABCs of Thinking and Feeling

Display 4.2 The ABC . . . Ds of Thinking and Feeling

Display 4.3 Either-Or, All-or-Nothing Thinking

Display 4.4 Disputing Unhelpful Thoughts or Beliefs

Display 4.6 Common Motivations for Residents' Difficult Behavior

Display 4.7 Common Caregiver Reactions to Residents' Difficult Behavior

Review the displays from Steps 1 and 2.

Step 4

Display 1.2 Pleasant Events

Display 2.5 Progressive Muscle Relaxation

Display 3.7 Mental Imagery

Display 4.8 Breathing-Focused Relaxation

Display 5.4 Common Situations in Which People Have Difficulty Expressing Themselves

Display 5.5 Using Assertive Communication in Relationships

Display 5.6 Setting Limits in Relationships

Review the displays from Steps 1, 2, and 3.

Step 5

Review all of the previously listed displays.

quency, intensity, or both, or it may be to shorten the duration of behavioral episodes. Continue using the techniques from Step 1.

In Step 2, also try to find at least one probable trigger or reinforcer of the behavior by using the ABCs of Behavior. To use the ABCs of Behavior, review Displays 3.1 and 3.3. Use photocopies of the ABCs of Behavior Observation Form in the appendix to determine probable triggers and reinforcers of one or two problem behaviors. Fill in the appropriate section of the form each time you see the behavior happening. Do this for up to 2 weeks or until you have an idea of the likely triggers and reinforcers. With behaviors that happen frequently, this process usually does not take longer than 2 weeks. For challenging behaviors that happen less frequently, it might take longer.

Step 3

In Step 3, the goal of the treatment plan may still be decreasing the behavior's frequency, intensity, or both or decreasing the duration of episodes. Based on findings from using the ABCs of Behavior Observation Form, your approaches to the problem can include changing what happens before the behavior occurs to avoid triggering it, changing what happens after the behavior occurs to avoid reinforcing it, or changing both the possible triggers and reinforcers. In Step 3, continue tracking the problem behavior with the ABCs of Behavior Observation Form. At the same time, continue using the Step 1 techniques. Often you will find that you need to fine-tune your use of these, not stop using them. If you have not found any possible triggers or reinforcers, perhaps the behavior happens too infrequently. Another possibility is that you are having difficulty using the ABCs of Behavior. Rereading the chapter on the ABCs of Behavior may help.

Also in Step 3, use the ABCs of Thinking and Feeling to help you manage the stress of working with this resident. Displays 4.1, 4.2, 4.3, and 4.4 can help you with this, and the ABCs of Thinking and Feeling form in the appendix can help you track these ABCs. Refer to Displays 4.6 and 4.7 as well to gain a better understanding of the resident's behavior.

Follow the revised treatment plan of Step 3 for the next 2 weeks. If you see improvement, great! Keep up the good work. If there is no positive change, if the problem has gotten worse, or if additional improvement would be good, go on to Step 4 of the treatment planning process.

Step 4

During Step 4, the goal may still be to decrease the behavior's frequency, intensity, or both or to decrease the length of duration for behavioral episodes. In Step 4, make at least one more change in the apparent triggers or reinforcers of the difficult behavior. Review the displays on stress management techniques to help you manage the stress of helping the resident with the difficult behavior: Displays 1.2, 2.5, 3.7, 4.8, 5.4, 5.5 and 5.6. In addition to using the stress management techniques that you found helpful in the past, now would be a good time to try a new one.

The approaches in Step 4 also include continuing to use Step 1's techniques, fine-tuning them as necessary. In addition, Step 4 calls for continuing the approach of using the ABCs of Behavior Observation Form.

Continue with Step 4 for the next 2 weeks. If improvement occurs, wonderful! Pay attention to what has been helpful, and give yourself credit for your work. Keep using what you have learned about the resident, about yourself, and about approaches that benefit you and the resident. If there has been no improvement or if the problem has gotten worse, it is time for Step 5.

Step 5

Step 5 involves gathering information from other people. Remember that it may be a good idea to talk with your supervisor throughout the treatment planning process when you are working with a resident who has a behavior problem. It is also good to talk with other staff members about how they interact with the resident. It is important to hear from staff members who have not had the same experience with the resident. Therefore, as a general rule, talk with at least five other staff members to find out about their interactions with the resident and their ways of addressing the resident's behavior. When you hear about others' experiences with the resident, pay close attention to what they do with the person rather than to such things as the staff members' gender, race, or age. Such characteristics are not likely to be the only things that trigger or reinforce a resident's positive or negative behavior.

Sometimes it is helpful to watch staff members with the resident when that person's behavior is less difficult. Paying attention to what these individuals do can help you learn beneficial, different ways of working with the resident. See Display 6.3 for an overview of the individual method.

Supervisor's Role in the Individual Method

In the individual treatment planning process, a supervisor can play an important role. Actively listening to the staff member is a vital part of this role. Other aspects of the supervisor's work in this role include using praise, compliments, and other social reinforcers regarding the staff member's efforts and successes; allowing the staff member to make choices; and using cooperative problem solving with the staff member. In addition, the supervisor upholds the mission of the nursing home to provide an environment that is sensitive and responsive to residents' needs, including psychological needs, by supporting staff–resident relationships.

Furthermore, it is important that employee evaluations assess familiarity with the basic skills for addressing problem behaviors. Supervisors themselves should also be evaluated. The appendix contains a Basic Psychological Skills Evaluation Form, which can be used as a part of routine, periodic performance evaluations of nursing home personnel.

If there is little success in treating a resident's behavior problem, the supervisor should be mindful that at least one individual is likely having difficulty using this book's principles and techniques. There are several things a supervisor can do

The Individual Method of Treatment Planning for a Resident's Behavior Problem

Step 1

Use good listening skills. As much as the resident will tolerate, work with him or her to determine what need motivates the behavior problem and what can be done about it. Frequently praise any of the resident's positive behaviors and provide the following: smiles, hugs, thumbs-up signs, or pats on the back. Reinforce effort. Remember that behavior change is sometimes gradual. Work toward realistic goals.

Note: If the resident engages in very disruptive attention-seeking behavior, go to him or her often — before the behavior starts. If you cannot reach the resident before the behavior starts, go to him or her before it escalates. Each time you go to the resident, help him or her with tasks for which assistance is requested, and support the resident's independent efforts, as much as he or she will tolerate. After 1–2 weeks, gradually lengthen the time between your visits — again, as much as the resident will tolerate.

Step 2

After 2 weeks, there may be significant improvement. If the behavior has gotten worse or additional improvement would be helpful, however, keep using the Step 1 techniques. As you do this over the next 2 weeks, pay careful attention to what happens right before and after the difficult behavior starts so you can uncover triggers and/or reinforcers.

Step 3

Change things that seem to trigger or reinforce the problem behavior. Often, ineffective use of the Step 1 techniques can be a trigger and/or reinforcer. For the next 2 weeks, keep using the Step 1 techniques, but make necessary changes in your use of them to eliminate or reduce triggers or reinforcers. If the behavior happens again, continue to look for triggers and reinforcers.

Note: If you often think that situations and people never change — that they are always bad — you are probably overstressed. Keep in mind that people do not do bad things all of the time, and it is very unlikely that a situation never changes.

(continued)

Step 4

Adjust one or two possible triggers or reinforcers. Maintain these adjustments over the next 2 weeks. During this time, benefit your work, relationships, and health by taking steps to manage stress. Make sure you take time for yourself every day—time to relax and to do things that you enjoy. Even little things such as talking with a friend, taking a walk, reading, or sitting quietly can be important.

Step 5

Talk with your supervisor about your work with the resident's behavior. In addition, talk with co-workers who experience the resident differently than you do. Watch those who have less trouble with the resident for ideas about what you can do.

Note: You can also begin doing the Step 5 activities during Step 1.

Caring for People with Challenging Behaviors: Essential Skills and Successful Strategies in Long-Term Care
© 2005 Stephen Weber Long. Published by Health Professions Press, Inc. (http://www.healthpropress.com).
All rights reserved.

in such a situation, many of which involve closer supervision. One possibility is individual supervision sessions with the staff member, focusing on the use of the techniques. It may be helpful to discuss this book one chapter at a time during supervision sessions. It can be important to let the staff member describe how using the techniques has or has not been effective in different situations with different people. This gives the staff member a chance to consider concrete ways of using the techniques and to think of ways he or she might use the techniques more successfully.

The supervisor can ensure that scheduling policies allow the staff member to attend training on addressing difficult resident behavior. He or she can work on removing institutional obstacles to the staff member's ability to attend such training opportunities.

Another tool a supervisor can use is the buddy system. A staff member who is having trouble with any aspect of his or her job, such as using effective techniques for addressing difficult behavior, can be assigned to work with another staff member who is more successful at it and perhaps has been on the job longer. Allowing staff members to mentor each other in areas in which they have strengths acknowledges and encourages important skills for working effectively in the nursing home.

If training and supervision do not efficiently help a staff member work well with a particular resident, it is best not to schedule him or her to work with that resident. With continued supervision, training, and personal growth (perhaps including psychotherapy), the staff member may develop the skills necessary to work with similar residents in the future.

In some cases, a staff member's personal obstacles will prevent him or her from using the best approaches effectively in particular situations, despite available training and supervision. For example, a staff member with a history of sexual abuse may not work well with male residents with dementia who expose themselves. Sometimes, a supervisor will be aware of such information about a staff member, but often not. This staff member may eventually work through the issues underlying the personal obstacles. However, this process may not happen quickly enough for the staff member to work well with a significant number of residents. When possible, supervisors should assign such staff members to other duties that make better use of their strengths. When reassignment is not possible, the supervisor and staff member might jointly explore the staff member's other employment opportunities and which supports he or she may have or need during the process of seeking new employment.

Sometimes it becomes apparent that a resident's problem behavior is a persistent, significant difficulty for other staff members as well. In such cases, it is time for the team method of treatment planning.

THE TEAM METHOD

When a resident's behavior problem is raised as an issue to be addressed by his or her formal, written treatment plan, the interdisciplinary treatment team serves an important function. This team usually includes members from different areas of expertise, such as physical medicine and rehabilitation, nutrition, chaplain services, internal medicine, social work, psychiatry, dentistry, nursing, and psychology. The team members can discuss their own experiences in working with the resident and can use active listening with each other. In addition, the members can acknowledge, show appreciation for, and offer praise and other social reinforcers for each other's ways of interacting with the resident that are in line with the nursing home's mission. They can discuss the basic techniques for addressing behavior problems, the best ways to implement them, potential obstacles to using them, and ideas for overcoming the obstacles. As a general rule, the team also can follow steps similar to those for the individual method to develop and document a treatment plan for problem behavior.

Like the individual method of treatment planning, the team method has five steps. Each step takes approximately 2 weeks. The following sections outline the steps for this method; the relevant displays are indicated in Display 6.2.

Step 1

As with the individual method, the goal of Step 1 is to decrease the behavior's frequency, intensity, or both or to shorten the duration of behavioral episodes. The problem is addressed by using active listening and cooperative problem solving with the resident. Other approaches include allowing the resident to make choices, using praise and other social reinforcers, and containing personal reactions to the resident's behavior. When significantly disruptive attention-seeking behavior is among a resident's problem behaviors, the stretching technique (see Display 3.5) should be used as part of Step 1.

In Step 1, treatment planning team members receive handouts on each approach. These are copies of the displays listed in Step 1 on Display 6.2. The person who distributes the handouts facilitates a review and brief discussion of their content. Discussion questions can include the following:

- "How might this handout's suggestions help—or not help—address the resident's behavior problems?"

- "What are your reactions to this handout's suggestions?"

- "How have these or similar ideas and techniques been helpful to you in other situations with different people?"

- "Why might these techniques be difficult to use, and how can we address these difficulties?"

An extended list of similar discussion questions appears in Display 6.4.

Encouraging team members to discuss their thoughts and reactions to the handouts' contents can be very helpful. Team members might not all agree with everything presented, but discussion can help deepen understanding of the psychological principles and techniques presented in each display distributed as a handout. Team members can also practice their active listening skills with each other during this discussion.

Discussion Questions

When using *Caring for People with Challenging Behaviors* displays as handouts (for supervising staff, as part of the team treatment process, or in formal educational settings), it is important to encourage discussion. Questions such as the following can help. Remember to promote the use of good listening skills during such sessions; this encourages participants to respond to questions or to raise their own questions regarding the ideas and techniques being considered.

- How might the handout's suggestions help — or not help — address a resident's problem behavior?

- What are your reactions to the handout's suggestions?

- How have these or similar ideas or techniques helped you in your interactions with residents?

- How have these or similar ideas or techniques helped you in your interactions with other people?

- What made these or similar ideas or techniques effective when you used them with this resident or other people?

- What might make it difficult to use these ideas or techniques with this resident?

- What can you do to address such factors?

- What else might make it less difficult to use these ideas or techniques?

Caring for People with Challenging Behaviors: Essential Skills and Successful Strategies in Long-Term Care
© 2005 Stephen Weber Long. Published by Health Professions Press, Inc. (http://www.healthpropress.com).
All rights reserved.

This process of review and discussion is intended to help the team members become familiar with, deepen their familiarity with, or renew their familiarity with the principles and techniques of addressing behavior problems in ways that will help them not only in their work with residents but also in supporting other staff members' use of these principles and techniques. In addition to their use in addressing residents' behavior problems, the review and discussion of handouts in this and other treatment planning steps can be counted toward the nursing home's requirements of ongoing training for staff.

In this step, supervisors or other designated individuals give copies of the displays describing the Step 1 techniques to staff members who work with or may work with the resident but who are not on the treatment planning team. When supervisors or others distribute the handouts, they briefly review the handouts with staff, allowing as much discussion of the material as possible. This is a good time to use active listening, praise, and other social reinforcers with staff members in ways that support the basic mission of the nursing home. The discussion can include the types of questions previously mentioned for use with the treatment planning team.

Use the techniques of Step 1 for 2 weeks. At the end of the 2 weeks, if there is no improvement, if the behavior has gotten worse, or if further improvement is desired, move on to Step 2.

Step 2

In Step 2, the goal is to reduce the behavior's intensity, frequency, or both or to reduce the duration of behavioral episodes. The approaches include continuing with the techniques of Step 1 and using the ABCs of Behavior Observation Form in the appendix to find possible triggers and reinforcers of the problem behavior. A third approach in Step 2 is for treatment team members to discuss the handouts listed in Step 2 of Display 6.2, using discussion questions such as those suggested in Display 6.4.

In Step 2, supervisors or other designated individuals distribute copies of Displays 3.1 and 3.3 to staff members who work with or may work with the resident but did not attend the treatment planning meeting. The handouts, which cover the ABCs of Behavior, are at least briefly discussed. This is part of ongoing education, training, and supervision. In this and all other similar discussions, it is again important to use active listening techniques as well as praise and other social reinforcers with staff members. It is also important to encourage staff to make choices in using the techniques that support the basic spirit of the treatment plan.

In Step 2, each episode of the problem behavior is reported to the charge nurse or other designated person who completes the ABCs of Behavior Observation Form, using Displays 3.1 and 3.3 as guides. This is done for the next 2 weeks. By the end of this 2-week period, the behavior may improve. If not, or if the behavior has gotten worse or additional improvement is desirable, it is time for Step 3.

Step 3

In Step 3, the goals continue to be to reduce the behavior's intensity, frequency, or both or to reduce the duration of behavioral episodes. Team members use information from the completed ABCs of Behavior Observation Forms to revise some approaches of the treatment plan. This information is applied to change triggers, reinforcers, or both. Even if possible triggers or reinforcers have not yet been determined, the team should go ahead with the rest of Step 3.

Another part of Step 3 is to continue with the techniques from Step 1. As mentioned previously, use of the techniques from Step 1 often needs to be fine-tuned, not discontinued.

In Step 3, it is time to pay closer attention to managing reactions to the resident. During a team meeting, the treatment planning team members review the ABCs of Thinking and Feeling. Each team member receives photocopies of the displays listed in Step 3 of Display 6.2. The meeting facilitator or another designated team member leads a review and brief discussion of each handout. See Display 6.4 for questions that can be used to further the review and discussion.

Part of Step 3 is ensuring that staff members who work with or may work with the resident but who are not on the interdisciplinary treatment planning team receive the Step 3 handouts, too. Immediate supervisors or other designated individuals distribute these, review them with staff, and facilitate brief discussion. Again, see Display 6.4 for questions to ask that can help the review and discussion of the handouts. This kind of discussion can be a very important way of providing necessary supervision in addressing a resident's difficult behavior.

If the behavior improves during the 2 weeks of Step 3, wonderful! Congratulations are in order for the direct care staff and the rest of the team. If there has been no positive change, if the problem has gotten worse, or if additional improvement is desired, go on to Step 4 in the treatment planning process.

Step 4

During Step 4, the goal is still to reduce the problem behavior's frequency, intensity, or both or to shorten behavioral episodes. Information about triggers or reinforcers of the behavior from the observation forms is used to revise approaches to the problem. Use of the techniques from Step 1 and the ABCs of Behavior Observation Form is continued. Step 4 adds the approach of offering stress management techniques to members of the treatment planning team and the staff members who work with the resident. The meeting facilitator or another designated person distributes photocopies of the displays listed in Step 4 of Display 6.2. Supervisors or other appropriate individuals provide these handouts to the staff members who work with or might work with the resident. The person distributing the handouts facilitates a brief team discussion about the handouts' content and reminds team members to review previously received handouts. The same type of discussion is held with other staff members who work directly with the resident. Step 1's questions for reviewing and discussing handouts can be used again here.

The Team Method of Treatment Planning for a Resident's Behavior Problem

The treatment planning team reviews and discusses the ideas listed in the following five steps. The same ideas are reviewed and discussed by staff members who work with or may work with the resident and who are not part of the treatment planning meeting. The team's review and discussion is led by the team facilitator or another designated person. Review and discussion among other staff members is facilitated by immediate supervisors or other appropriate people.

Step 1

Review and discuss listening skills, praise and other social reinforcers, cooperative problem solving, and — in cases of disruptive attention-seeking behavior — techniques for helping the resident stretch his or her ability to tolerate appropriate intervals without being a focus of attention. In the written treatment plan, note that these approaches will be used to address the resident's difficult behavior. After 2 weeks of following Step 1, go to Step 2.

Step 2

Review and discuss how behaviors are triggered and reinforced. Continue to use the techniques from Step 1. Ensure that episodes of the problem behavior are reported to the charge nurse or other designated person, who notes the behavior as well as what happened just before the behavior occurred, once the behavior started, and just as the behavior ended. After 2 weeks, go to Step 3.

Step 3

Review and discuss the importance of managing one's own reactions to the resident. Continue with the techniques from Step 1. Adjust the possible triggers and reinforcers found in Step 2. Update the written care plan to show any adjustments. Continue the search for possible triggers and reinforcers if none have been found yet. Ensure that episodes of the problem behavior continue to be reported to the charge nurse or other designated person, who records all pertinent details. After 2 weeks, go to Step 4.

Step 4

Review and discuss additional ways of dealing with one's own reactions to the resident and his or her behavior. Continue using the techniques from Step 1. Change at least one

(continued)

trigger or reinforcer of the problem behavior. Note that change on the written care plan. Continue trying to uncover triggers and reinforcers if none have been found yet. Ensure that episodes of the behavior continue to be reported to the charge nurse or other designated person, who records the pertinent details. After 2 weeks, go to Step 5.

Step 5

If there has been no improvement by this time and the problem behavior is of strong or very strong intensity (i.e., 4 or 5 on the scale presented in Display 6.1), engage in team discussion of possible root causes (e.g., institutional obstacles). Discuss these issues with the nursing home administration, and formulate a plan for addressing possible root causes.

Caring for People with Challenging Behaviors: Essential Skills and Successful Strategies in Long-Term Care

Continue with Step 4 for the next 2 weeks. If there has been improvement, great! The efforts of the team and direct care staff have paid off. If further improvement is desirable, the team should use what it has found in the treatment planning process to set new goals and then should adjust the approaches as needed. If there has been no improvement or the behavior has gotten worse, however, the team should go on to Step 5.

Step 5

Step 5 calls for the team to discuss possible root causes of the obstacles to effectively addressing the resident's problem behavior. In this discussion, team members focus on ideas about what is needed to most effectively address the resident's problem behavior. Things that are deemed necessary but unavailable are related to the root causes. The root causes themselves may most helpfully be looked at as any processes that prevent what is needed from being obtained. The goal of looking for root causes is not looking to blame any particular person; rather, it is looking at general practices and policies that interfere with solutions to the problems presented by a resident's behavior. Sometimes team members will not discern the root causes, but it is helpful for them to at least list the things they believe might be needed to effectively address the resident's problem.

Following this discussion, ideas about what things are needed, possible obstacles to obtaining them, and possible steps to begin addressing the obstacles can be discussed with the nursing home's administrative staff. Such dialogue uncovers an approach to addressing the obstacles, and the approach can then be followed in a flexible manner that allows for responding to feedback from staff, residents, residents' family members or significant others, and the wider community. See Display 6.5 for a summary of the team approach to treatment planning.

SUMMARY

This chapter described treatment planning for behavior problems. Two methods of treatment planning were discussed: an individual approach that can guide individual staff members in addressing problem behaviors and a team approach to use when a resident's behavior is a significant difficulty that is not being sufficiently addressed by the individual approach. Both approaches have five steps, and each step is based on previous chapters of this book.

Finally, this chapter discussed prevention as an approach to the treatment of behavior problems. An ongoing process to familiarize, refamiliarize, or deepen familiarity with the techniques and principles presented in *Caring for People with Challenging Behaviors* can aid in creating and supporting a nursing home culture that is effective in preventing or limiting the intensity of many behavior problems. (See the For the Reader section at the beginning of the book for a detailed approach to furthering such a culture in long-term care settings.)

Bibliography

Aron, L. (1996). *A meeting of minds: Mutuality in psychoanalysis.* Hillsdale, NJ: The Analytic Press.

Aronson, M. (1956, January). Psychiatric management of disturbed behavior in a home for the aged. *Geriatrics, 39*–43.

Barns, E.K., Sack, A., & Shore, H. (1973, Winter). Guidelines to treatment approaches: Modalities for use with the aged. *The Gerontologist,* 513–527.

Bouklas, G. (1997). *Psychotherapy with the elderly: Becoming Methuselah's echo.* Northvale, NJ: Jason Aronson.

Brandtstadter, J., & Baltes-Gotz, B. (1990). Personal control over development and quality of life perspectives in adulthood. In P.B. Baltes & M.M. Baltes (Eds.), *Successful aging* (pp. 197–224). Cambridge, England: Cambridge University Press.

Burgio, L.D., & Burgio, K.L. (1986). Behavioral gerontology: Application of behavioral methods to problems of older adults. *Journal of Applied Behavior Analysis, 19,* 321–328.

Chafetz, P.K. (1996). Behavioral management of secondary symptoms of dementia. In R.L. Dippel & J.T. Hutton (Eds.), *Caring for the Alzheimer patient: A practical guide* (pp. 123–133). Amherst, NY: Prometheus Books.

Cohler, B.J. (1998). Psychoanalysis and the life course: Development and intervention. In I.H. Nordhus, G.R. VandenBos, S. Berg, & P. Fromholt (Eds.), *Clinical geropsychology* (pp. 79–108). Washington, DC: American Psychological Association.

Cohn, M.D., Smyer, M.A., & Horgas, A.L. (1994). *The ABCs of behavior change: Skills for working with behavior problems in nursing homes.* State College, PA: Ventura Publishing.

Colarusso, C.A., & Nemiroff, R.A. (1981). *Adult development.* New York: Plenum Press.

Dinkmeyer, D., McKay, G.D., McKay, J.L., & Dinkmeyer, D. Jr. (1998). *Parenting teens: Systematic training for effective parenting.* Circle Pines, MN: AGS Publishing.

Feil, N. (2002). *The Validation breakthrough: Simple techniques for communicating with people with "Alzheimer's-type dementia"* (2nd ed.). Baltimore: Health Professions Press.

Finkel, S.I. (1993). Diagnosis and treatment of delirium in the nursing home. In P.A. Szwabo & G.T. Grossberg (Eds.), *Problem behaviors in long-term care: Recognition, diagnosis, and treatment* (pp. 110–121). New York: Springer-Verlag.

Gallagher-Thompson, D., Ossindale, C., & Thompson, L.W. (1999). *Coping with caregiving: A class for family caregivers.* Unpublished manuscript, Veterans Administration Palo Alto Healthcare System and Stanford University School of Medicine.

Gatz, M. (2000). Variations on depression in later life. In S.H. Qualls & N. Abeles (Eds.), *Psychology and the aging revolution: How we adapt to longer life* (pp. 239–254). Washington, DC: American Psychological Association.

Gubrium, J.F. (1997). *Living and dying at Murray Manor.* Charlottesville: The University of Virginia Press.

Gwyther, L.P. (1986, May). Treating behavior as a symptom of illness. *Provider,* 18–21.

Henderson, J.N. (1995). The culture of care in a nursing home: Effects of a medicalized model of long term care. In J.N. Henderson & M.D. Vesperi (Eds.), *The culture of long term care: Nursing home ethnography* (pp. 37–54). Westport, CT: Bergin & Garvey.

Jencks, S.F., & Clauser, S.B. (1991). Improving nursing home care through training and job redesign. *The Gerontologist, 32*(2), 327–333.

Jenike, M. (1988). Depression and other psychiatric disorders. In M.S. Albert & M.B. Moss (Eds.), *Geriatric neuropsychology* (pp. 115–144). New York: The Guilford Press.

Joiner, T.E. (2000). Depression: Current developments and controversies. In S.H. Qualls & N. Abeles (Eds.), *Psychology and the aging revolution: How we adapt to longer life* (pp. 223–237). Washington, DC: American Psychological Association.

Karon, B.P., & VanderBos, G.R. (1998). Schizophrenia and psychosis in elderly populations. In I.H. Nordhus, G.R. VandenBos, S. Berg, & P. Fromholt (Eds.), *Clinical geropsychology* (pp. 219–227). Washington, DC: American Psychological Association.

Kasl-Godley, J.E., Gatz, M., & Fiske, A. (1998). Depression and depressive symptoms in old age. In I.H. Nordhus, G.R. VandenBos, S. Berg, & P. Fromholt (Eds.), *Clinical geropsychology* (pp. 211–217). Washington, DC: American Psychological Association.

Keane, B., & Dixon, C. (2001). *Caring for people with behavior problems: A basic, practical text for nurses, health workers and others who are learning to manage difficult behaviors.* Melbourne, Australia: Ausmed Publications.

Kübler-Ross, E. (1969). *On death and dying: What the dying have to teach doctors, nurses, clergy, and their own families.* New York: Collier Books.

Lach, H.W. (1993). Use of physical restraints and options. In P.A. Szwabo & G.T. Grossberg (Eds.), *Problem behaviors in long-term care: Recognition, diagnosis, and treatment* (pp. 176–187). New York: Springer-Verlag.

Lazarus, R.S. (1998). Coping with aging: Individuality as a key to understanding. In I.H. Nordhus, G.R. VandenBos, S. Berg, & P. Fromholt (Eds.), *Clinical geropsychology* (pp. 109–127). Washington, DC: American Psychological Association.

Lewinsohn, P.M., Antonuccio, D.O., Brechenridge, J.S., & Teri, L. (1984). *The coping with depression course.* Eugene, OR: Castalia Publishing Company.

Lewinsohn, P.M., Muñoz, R.F., Youngren, M.A., & Zeiss, A.M. (1986). *Control your depression: Reducing depression through learning self-control techniques, relaxation training, pleasant activities, social skills, constructed thinking, planning ahead, and more.* New York: Fireside.

Lipson, S. (1994). The restraint-free approach to behavior problems in the nursing home. *Maryland Medical Journal, 43*(2), 155–157.

Lomranz, J. (1991). Mental health in homes for the aged and the clinical psychology of aging: Implementation of a model service. *Clinical Gerontologist, 10*(3), 47–72.

Mahoney, E.K., Volicer, L., & Hurley, A.C. (2000). *Management of challenging behaviors in dementia.* Baltimore: Health Professions Press.

McCleary, R.W. (1992). *Conversing with uncertainty: Practicing psychotherapy in a hospital setting.* Hillsdale, NJ: The Analytic Press.

Meyers, B.S., & Cahenzi, C.T. (1993). Psychotropics in the extended care facility. In P.A. Szwabo & G.T. Grossberg (Eds.), *Problem behaviors in long-term care: Recognition, diagnosis, and treatment* (pp. 81–93). New York: Springer-Verlag.

Mitchell, S.A., & Black, M.J. (1995). *Freud and beyond: A history of modern psychoanalytic thought.* New York: Basic Books.

Morley, J.E., & Miller, D.K. (1993). Behavioral concomitants of common medical disorders. In P.A. Szwabo & G.T. Grossberg (Eds.), *Problem behaviors in long-term care: Recognition, diagnosis, and treatment* (pp. 97–109). New York: Springer-Verlag.

Nelson, J. (1995, May). The influence of environmental factors in incidents of disruptive behavior. *Journal of Gerontological Nursing,* 19–24.

Norcross, J.C., & Knight, B.G. (2000). Psychotherapy and aging in the 21st century: Integrative themes. In S.H. Qualls & N. Abeles (Eds.), *Psychology and the aging revolution: How we adapt to longer life* (pp. 259–286). Washington, DC: American Psychological Association.

Pinkston, E., & Linsk, N.L. (1984). *Care of the elderly: A family approach.* New York: Pergamon Press.

Ray, W.A., Taylor, J.A., Lichtenstein, M.J., Meador, K.G., Stovdemire, A., Lipton, B., & Blazer, D. (1991). Managing behavior problems in nursing home residents. *Contemporary Management in Internal Medicine, 1,* 71–112.

Ray, W.A., Taylor, J.A., Meador, K.G., Lichtenstein, M.J., Griffin, M.R., Fought, R., Adams, M.L., & Blazer, D.G. (1993). Reducing antipsychotic drug use in nursing homes: A controlled trial of provider education. *Archives of Internal Medicine, 153,* 713–721.

Rogers, J.C., Holm, M.B., Burgio, L.D., Granieri, E., Hsu, C., Hardin, M., & McDowell, B.J. (1999). Improving morning care routines of nursing home residents with dementia. *Journal of the American Geriatrics Society, 47,* 1049–1057.

Romeis, J.C. (1993). Problem behaviors among younger adult nursing home residents. In P.A. Szwabo & G.T. Grossberg (Eds.), *Problem behaviors in long-term care: Recognition, diagnosis, and treatment* (pp. 21–31). New York: Springer-Verlag.

Rovner, B.W., Lucas-Blaustein, J., Folstein, M.F., & Smith, S.W. (1990). Stability over one year in patients admitted to a nursing home dementia unit. *International Journal of Geriatric Psychiatry, 5,* 77–82.

Ryan, R.M., & LaGuardia, J.G. (2000). What is being optimized?: Self-determination theory and basic psychological needs. In S.H. Qualls & N. Abeles (Eds.), *Psychology and the aging revolution: How we adapt to longer life* (pp. 145–172). Washington, DC: American Psychological Association.

Scogin, F.R. (1998). Anxiety in old age. In I.H. Nordhus, G.R. VandenBos, S. Berg, & P. Fromholt (Eds.), *Clinical geropsychology* (pp. 205–209). Washington, DC: American Psychological Association.

Sky, A.J., & Grossberg, G.T., (1993). Aggressive behaviors and chemical restraints. In P.A. Szwabo & G.T. Grossberg (Eds.), *Problem behaviors in long-term care: Recognition, diagnosis, and treatment* (pp. 188–200). New York: Springer-Verlag.

Slochower, J.A. (1996). *Holding and psychoanalysis: A relational perspective.* Hillsdale, NJ: The Analytic Press.

Smyer, M.A., Brannon, D., & Cohn, M. (1992). Improving nursing home care through training and job redesign. *The Gerontologist, 32*(2), 327–333.

Smyer, M.A., & Downs, M.G. (1995). Psychopharmacology: An essential element in educating clinical psychologists for working with older adults. In B.G. Knight, L. Teri, P. Wohlford, & J. Santos (Eds.), *Mental health services for older adults: Implications for training and practice in geropsychology* (pp. 73–83). Washington, DC: American Psychological Association.

Snowdon, J. (1993). Mental health in nursing homes: Perspectives on the use of medications. *Drugs and Aging, 3*(2), 122–130.

Solomon, K. (1993). Behavioral and psychotherapeutic interventions with residents in long-term care institutions. In P.A. Szwabo & G.T. Grossberg (Eds.), *Problem behaviors in long-term care: Recognition, diagnosis, and treatment* (pp. 147–162). New York: Springer-Verlag.

Spayd, S.C., & Smyer, M.A. (1996). Psychological interventions in nursing homes. In S.H. Zarit & B.G. Knight (Eds.), *A guide to psychotherapy and aging* (pp. 241–268). Washington, DC: American Psychological Association.

Stevens, A.B., Burgio, L.D., Bailey, E., Burgio, K.L., Paul, P., Capilouto, E., Nicovich, P., & Hale, G. (1998). Teaching and maintaining behavior management skills with nursing assistants in a nursing home. *The Gerontologist, 38*(3), 379–384.

Streim, J.E., & Katz, I.R. (1994). Federal regulations and the care of patients with dementia in the nursing home. *Medical Clinics of North America, 78*(4), 895–909.

Szwabo, P.A., & Boesch, K.R. (1993). Impact of personality and personality disorders in the elderly. In P.A. Szwabo & G.T. Grossberg (Eds.), *Problem behaviors in long-term care: Recognition, diagnosis, and treatment* (pp. 59–69). New York: Springer-Verlag.

Taylor, R.L. (1990). *Distinguishing psychological from organic disorders: Screening for psychological masquerade.* New York: Springer-Verlag.

Teri, L. (1992). Non-pharmacological approaches to management of patient behavior: A focus on behavioral interventions for depression in dementia. In G. Gutman (Ed.), *Shelter and care of persons with dementia* (pp. 101–113). Vancouver, British Columbia, Canada: Simon Fraser University, The Gerontology Research Centre.

Teri, L., & Umoto, J.M. (1991). Reducing excess disability in dementia patients: Training caregivers to manage patient depression. *Clinical Gerontologist, 10*(4), 49–63.

Veterans Health Administration's Employee Education System. (2001). *Prevention and management of disruptive behavior.* Washington, DC: Veteran's Administration Office of Occupational Safety and Health.

Wachtel, P.L. (1997). *Psychoanalysis, behavior therapy, and the relational world.* Washington, DC: American Psychological Association.

Whitbourne, S.K. (1998). Physical changes in the aging individual: Clinical implications. In

I.H. Nordhus, G.R. VandenBos, S. Berg, & P. Fromholt (Eds.), *Clinical geropsychology* (pp. 79–108). Washington DC: American Psychological Association.

Zarit, S.H. (1996). Ethical considerations in the treatment of older adults. In S.H. Zarit & B.G. Knight (Eds.), *A guide to psychotherapy and aging* (pp. 269–284). Washington, DC: American Psychological Association.

Zarit, S.H., Dolan, M.M., & Leitsch, S.A. (1998). Interventions in nursing homes and alternate living settings. In I.H. Nordhus, G.R. VandenBos, S. Berg, & P. Fromholt (Eds.), *Clinical geropsychology* (pp. 329–343). Washington, DC: American Psychological Association.

Blank Forms

Top 10 Pleasant Events List
Pleasant Events Tracking Form
New Top 10 Pleasant Events List
ABCs of Behavior Observation Form
ABCs of Thinking and Feeling Form
Basic Psychological Skills Evaluation Form

Top 10 Pleasant Events List

1. _____

2. _____

3. _____

4. _____

5. _____

6. _____

7. _____

8. _____

9. _____

10. _____

List 10 small, pleasant activities you like to do. Make sure that the activities are realistic, "do-able" things such as taking a short walk, talking with a friend, sitting alone quietly, holding hands with a loved one, or watching a favorite television program.

Include activities that you do not already do often. Rank the items, placing the one that is most important to you at the top of the list.

Pleasant Events Tracking Form

Pleasant Events	Day & Date	Day & Date	Day & Date	Day & Date	Day & Date	Day & Date	Day & Date
1							
2							
3							
4							
5							
6							
7							
8							
9							
10							
Totals for each day							

List your top 10 pleasant events in the lefthand column. Record the day and date you start tracking at the top of the next column. Record the day and date of the following 6 days over the remaining columns.

In the column below each day and date, place a check mark in the appropriate box when one of your pleasant activities has occurred. Even if you experience the same event numerous times in one day, place only one check mark in the box. For example, if one of your pleasant events is reading the newspaper, only check the corresponding activity and date box one time, even if you sit down to read the paper four times that day.

At the end of each day, count the number of check marks in that day's column. Record the number of check marks for that day in the box at the bottom of the column.

Your goal may be to have more of your top 10 pleasant events each day than recorded on the list.

New Top 10 Pleasant Events List

1. _____

2. _____

3. _____

4. _____

5. _____

6. _____

7. _____

8. _____

9. _____

10. _____

After a week of tracking your top 10 pleasant events, use this form to update your list. Replace anything from the previous list that you were not able to do. Or leave some of these items on the list for one more week if you think that you will be more able to do them now.

Use a copy of this form each week. Remove items from earlier Top 10 Lists that were unrealistic. Remove other activities that have become routine—that is, the ones that you now experience very often. Substitute do-able pleasant activities that you do not already do often. Rank the items, beginning with the one that you value most. Use the Pleasant Events Tracking Form to tally how many of your new Top 10 pleasant events you have each week.

ABCs of Behavior Observation Form

Date:	Time:	
A **Antecedent**	**B** **Behavior**	**C** **Consequence**

Date:	Time:	
A **Antecedent**	**B** **Behavior**	**C** **Consequence**

Date:	Time:	
A **Antecedent**	**B** **Behavior**	**C** **Consequence**

ABCs of Thinking and Feeling Form

Date:			
A **Activating Event**	**B** **Beliefs/Thoughts**	**C** **Emotional** **Consequences**	**D** **Disputing** **Beliefs/Thoughts**

Basic Psychological Skills Evaluation Form

Staff member: _____

Supervisor: _____ Date: _____

Instructions for the supervisor: This chart delineates 14 skills for evaluation. The first 12 skills relate to the staff member's work with residents and should be evaluated according to his or her application of them with residents who engage in challenging behavior and routinely with all residents. (For your reference, descriptions of all 14 skill areas follow the chart.) Use these keys for indicating the staff member's ability in each area:

Performance rating:
E = Excellent
G = Good
S = Satisfactory
I = Improving/Needs Improvement

Assessment based on:
R = Staff member's report
D = Documentation
O = Observation by supervisor

Skills assessed	Performance rating (Circle one)				Assessment based on (Circle all that apply)		
1. Uses listening skills	E	G	S	I	R	D	O
2. Allows residents to make choices	E	G	S	I	R	D	O
3. Determines triggers and reinforcers of difficult behavior	E	G	S	I	R	D	O
4. Uses social reinforcers to encourage positive behaviors	E	G	S	I	R	D	O
5. Encourages residents to be actively involved in problem solving (as much as residents are able)	E	G	S	I	R	D	O
6. Effectively addresses attention-seeking behavior that is disruptive	E	G	S	I	R	D	O
7. Responds well to angry, hostile, or agitated behavior	E	G	S	I	R	D	O
8. Avoids negative approaches to difficult behaviors	E	G	S	I	R	D	O
9. Sets realistic goals for addressing difficult behaviors	E	G	S	I	R	D	O

10. Considers how difficult behaviors may be signs of psychological distress	E	G	S	I		R	D	O
11. Consults with others when having difficulty addressing a problem behavior	E	G	S	I		R	D	O
12. Spends at least 2–5 minutes daily visiting with each assigned or scheduled resident	E	G	S	I		R	D	O
13. Recognizes the importance of managing his or her own stress	E	G	S	I		R	D	O
14. Identifies potentially helpful methods of coping with stress that affects work performance	E	G	S	I		R	D	O

Comments:

Descriptions of the 14 Basic Psychological Skills

1. Uses listening skills: The staff member shows signs of paying attention, such as stopping whatever he or she is doing, making eye contact, nodding his or her head, and so forth. He or she accepts and names residents' feelings and accurately restates to residents what they say.

2. Allows residents to make choices: The staff member uses open-ended questions (e.g., "When would you like to go to bed?") with residents who are interested in and able to make decisions. He or she uses limited-choice questions (e.g., "I can help you now or after your television program. Which would you prefer?") with residents who are interested in and able to make decisions and with residents who have difficulty with open-ended questions because of confusion, bad moods, or low motivation. The staff member uses open-ended questions more often than limited-choice questions with residents who are comfortable with and able to respond to them. He or she gives clear, step-by-step explanations to residents who are very confused or do not respond to questions. The staff member recognizes resistance or agitation at such times as possible indications of the resident's choice to reject what is being done. The staff member respects this choice as long as it does not pose risks to the well-being and safety of the resident or others.

3. Determines triggers and reinforcers of difficult behavior: The staff member examines episodes of residents' difficult behavior to understand what triggers the difficult behavior and, if the behavior continues or worsens, what reinforces it.

4. Uses social reinforcers to encourage positive behaviors: The staff member uses praise, compliments, and acknowledgment of residents' efforts and positive or improved behaviors. He or she makes at least four positive comments to a resident for every one comment on a negative behavior.

5. Encourages residents to be actively involved in problem solving (as much as residents are able): The staff member listens to residents' points of view regarding problems. He or she asks residents what has usually resolved these or similar problems in the past, then works with residents to select possible solutions.

6. Effectively addresses attention-seeking behavior that is disruptive: The staff member works to meet residents' needs for attention and works toward gradual improvement in their abilities to tolerate longer periods of independence.

7. Responds well to angry, hostile, or agitated behavior: The staff member is alert to signs that the resident is becoming agitated (e.g., shouting demands, making threats). He or she gives residents space at such times. The staff member may describe limited choices for agitated residents, such as, "If you speak more calmly to me, I'll try to help you" or "If you shout at me again, I'll leave you on your own for about 15 minutes." (The staff member only does the latter if leaving does not put anyone at immediate risk of harm.) The staff member avoids getting defensive or counteraggressive.

Caring for People with Challenging Behaviors: Essential Skills and Successful Strategies in Long-Term Care
© 2005 Stephen Weber Long. Published by Health Professions Press, Inc. (http://www.healthpropress.com).
All rights reserved.

8. Avoids negative approaches to difficult behaviors: The staff member avoids all of the following: nagging; arguing; making repeated demands; making threats; retaliating; withholding privileges; scolding; reprimanding; punishing; insisting that things are not the way residents see them; laughing at residents; making residents the butt of jokes; engaging in power struggles; and showing annoyance, frustration, or anger. He or she also avoids labeling difficult or agitated behavior as "unpredictable" or "unprovoked" and instead tries to identify and address triggers and reinforcers. The staff member acts in ways that model positive reactions to difficult circumstances and feelings.

9. Sets realistic goals for addressing difficult behaviors: The staff member realizes that behavior change is often gradual. He or she remembers that improvement is evident when difficult behaviors lessen in frequency or intensity or when behavioral episodes shorten. He or she recognizes that these changes can take longer with residents with histories of long-established behavior patterns. He or she avoids overgeneralizing (e.g., seeing a resident who engages in a challenging behavior as *always* behaving in difficult ways) and "catastrophizing" (e.g., seeing unpleasant, unfortunate behavior as *completely* terrible, horrible, or dangerous).

10. Considers how difficult behaviors may be signs of psychological distress: The staff member examines whether problem behaviors are motivated by unmet needs (e.g., the need for attention or for a sense of control, power, or effectiveness). He or she helps residents meet those needs.

11. Consults with others when having difficulty addressing a problem behavior: The staff member uses his or her supervisor and other staff members as resources. He or she talks to and watches others who have more success in working with problem behaviors or with a particular resident. The staff member uses this information to find new ways of addressing persistent problems.

12. Spends at least 2–5 minutes daily visiting with each assigned or scheduled resident: The staff member spends time with residents each day. If chatting with residents, he or she emphasizes active listening. During this time, the staff member engages in activities that residents initiate or prefer (e.g., watching television, walking, people watching, sitting in the sun, listening to music, discussing news).

13. Recognizes the importance of managing his or her own stress: The staff member recognizes that his or her ability to manage stress affects how well he or she uses basic skills. He or she sees lack of improvement in residents' problem behaviors as a possible sign that his or her stress level is interfering with effective use of basic skills.

14. Identifies potentially helpful methods of coping with stress that affects work performance: The staff member can state how stress may be better managed by strategies such as engaging in teamwork, being open to different approaches to problems, and being open to different ways of thinking about problems that have considerable support in clinical and research literature.

Index

DOWNLOAD THE COMPANION POSTER SERIES!

Print-ready PDF files of each of these 12 colorful, instructive posters are available for free download at http://www.healthpropress.com/posterseries.

Use these posters to teach and remind your staff about effective behavioral intervention.

Book Display No.	Poster Title
1.1	Understanding Causes of Behavior Problems Among Nursing Home Residents
2.1	Active Listening
2.2	Allowing Choices
2.3	Using Praise, Compliments, and Acknowledgment
2.4	Things to Avoid When Trying to Encourage Positive Behavior
3.1	The ABCs of Behavior
3.2	Holding On: Dealing with Reactions to Problem Behaviors
3.4	Realistic Goals for Residents' Problem Behaviors
3.6	Cooperative Problem Solving
4.5	Avoiding Physical Harm by a Resident
4.7	Common Caregiver Reactions to Residents' Difficult Behavior
5.6	Setting Limits in Relationships

HPP
Health Professions Press

Health Professions Press
P.O. Box 10624, Baltimore, MD 21285-0624
Toll-Free: (888) 337-8808 • Fax: (410) 337-8539
www.healthpropress.com